∿∿∿∿∿∿∿∿∿∿∿∿∿∿∿∿∿∿∿

Willis Stories

Written by

Keith Willis

∿∿∿∿∿∿∿∿∿∿∿∿∿∿∿∿∿∿∿

3

Bed and Breakfast

Bed and breakfast owners in Las Cruces, southern New Mexico, invited a Fort Selden park ranger to come and do a soldier presentation for their guests. I accepted and got dressed in 1880s wooly soldier garb. I grabbed a couple of black-powder rifles and a sack of gear and headed out in a state pickup truck.

I located the bed and breakfast and found a parking spot about a block away. I collected my guns and equipment and walked to the bed and breakfast. The owners ushered me in to a waiting group of about fifteen adults. I spent fifteen minutes talking about the history of the area and of Fort Selden and the surrounding Indian tribes.

What I did not know was that a neighbor lady had seen me walking along the sidewalk in strange clothes carrying two guns. She called the cops. There was a bank a couple of blocks away. The cops were now mobilizing and the local news station had learned of the incident over the police radio frequency.

I finished my history and soldier presentation and suggested we all go out back for a demonstration of the guns. A couple of ladies headed to the bathroom and the other guests carried chairs outside. I showed them a Sharps carbine and a long barrel 58 caliber rifle. Then I loaded a black powder cartridge into the long rifle (no lead bullet), put on a firing cap, aimed at the sky, and fired. There was a loud bang. A big puff of black smoke blew out of the barrel, and everybody was pleased.

The police patrolling through the neighborhood now had a clue where the stranger with the guns was because they heard the bang. A lady came from the bathroom and said she didn't get to see the first shot; could I shoot another? I said "sure" and loaded another powder cartridge into the rifle and fired it. This resulted in another loud bang and everybody was happy.

A different lady headed back inside the bed and breakfast to go to the bathroom. About a minute later she reappeared around the outside of the building. She walked over and whispered in my ear that the police out front would like to speak with me. I lowered my rifle in my left hand and headed that way when a husky police sergeant stepped around the corner of the building, his pistol drawn and pointed in the air. His forehead showed sweat so he was nervous.

I asked what he was doing and he breathed a big sigh of relief. He told me this was the first time he had drawn his gun while on duty. I looked around the side of the house to the street out front, and there were cops and cop cars everywhere. Creeping slowly toward me was a nervous news reporter with a camera pointed at me. Sweat was running down his forehead. When he got close, he asked what I was doing. I told him I was a park ranger from Fort Selden doing a soldier demonstration at the bed and breakfast. I told him that I didn't know we weren't supposed to shoot guns inside the city limits so I was sorry about that.

Then I walked to the front yard of the building to get a better view of all of the commotion. The camera guy followed along beside me with film still rolling. I had to chuckle at all the cops and cop cars everywhere.

I then went back to the rear of the bed and breakfast where the guests were still gathered and told them the demonstration was over. A couple of ladies helped me carry the guns back to my truck.

The next day at Fort Selden one of the bed and breakfast visitors came to see me. She filled me in on the previous evening's TV news. The story of the day was the police manhunt for a stranger carrying guns near the bank. The largest manhunt in Las Cruces in the past decade turned out to be a park ranger from Fort Selden. A false alarm. Some of the bed and breakfast guests had gotten on TV. This was big entertainment for them.

I asked the lady if I came across the news as a bad guy and she said no. It was just a simple mistake.

One footnote to this story came about a month later when the news reporter showed up at Fort Selden during a dress reenactment day. I recognized him and we shared some laughs. He told me that more than twenty cop cars had surrounded the bed and breakfast during the soldier incident, and a SWAT sniper, after locating my position, had put me in his crosshairs to see if I was a threat to the bed and breakfast guests.

Me and Boris

I was working at Fort Selden State Monument in New Mexico in the late 1980s. We received a phone call one morning and were told that a VIP group was headed our way. Half an hour later, Boris Yeltsin showed up with a small group that included a tour guide and an interpreter. Yeltsin was visiting the School of Mines College in nearby Las Cruces. He wasn't yet President of Russia.

I took the group out behind the museum and gave them a brief history of the fort and soldiers who were stationed here in the 1800s. When talking to people who don't speak English, you stick to basics and keep it short.

Then I got a black powder rifle, intending to do a demo firing. I rammed a powder cartridge down the barrel (no lead bullet), put on a firing cap, and cocked the hammer. On a whim, I decided to let Boris shoot the gun. He gave a big smile, took the gun, put it on his shoulder, aimed it up in the air, and pulled the trigger. Boom! This boom was bigger than usual.

Everyone was startled by the big boom, including me. Boris showed a big smile and said "Da", meaning approval. He liked it. A man of action, without fear.

Another ranger then came and gave the VIP group a walking tour around the old adobe fort ruins. Then they left.

Later I figured out why the Boris gunshot had been so loud. I remembered loading the gun the previous day but hadn't fired it. When I loaded the gun for Boris, I was putting one powder load on top of another. Without a lead bullet in the barrel, there was no harm done. There was just a big bang twice as loud as usual with twice the powder blasting out the end of the gun.

Boris enjoyed the big bang. It woke everybody up. I'm sure he remembered it for a while.

Fastest Dog in the West

I was working in California in the 1990s, living in a motorhome parked near a roadway. One evening at dusk I heard a car come to a sudden stop on the road and then a loud thump. Another car came along and stopped. People got out of their cars and started talking so I decided to go investigate.

I went outside and walked to the roadway where a couple of cars were parked off the shoulder. Several people were gathered around, looking down at the road. A lady was gently sobbing. She was the driver of the first car. Car lights were on so I could see a black dog lying motionless on the pavement. Everybody there assumed the dog was dead because he wasn't moving.

Somebody got a flashlight and shined it on the dog. He was medium-sized. His eyes moved a little when the flashlight hit him so he wasn't dead yet, but pretty close.

Nobody knew what to do. The dog wasn't trying to move. I told the people I could put the dog out of his misery if they were okay with that.

Nobody objected so I went to get a gun from my RV. I got a loaded rifle and a flashlight and returned. By this time darkness had set in.

I asked the people to move to my side. I would aim away from us at the dog's head. I put the flashlight on him and his eyes rolled a little. Then I pointed the rifle through the light toward his head.

In the next instant, the dog was gone. He had vanished. Just a couple of seconds earlier he was lying motionless on the road, presumably near death. Now he was nowhere to be seen.

I listened but couldn't hear anything. I looked in the direction I thought the dog went. Nothing. I looked at the other people there. They were looking around and listening, too. They looked at me. The only thing I heard when the dog disappeared was a brief scratching of his toenails on the pavement.

Everybody nodded their heads in approval. The dog just needed some coaxing. The lady stopped crying. We all went back to our business.

I still marvel at how fast that dog disappeared. Think what he could do if he wasn't injured.

Bad Gas

Fort Sumner in eastern New Mexico was established in the late 1800s as a Navajo Indian Reservation. A state monument is there today to honor the Indians who lived there. It is also the site where Billy the Kid was shot and buried.

Daily visitation to the monument is low. On a day in the late 1980s, a family drove to see the monument and the museum. The park ranger greeted the travelers and began telling the group about the history of the site. Then it happened. The park ranger accidentally farted. It was one of those unsuspecting farts; it just slipped out without warning. And worse, it was pretty loud and it smelled.

Everybody heard it and soon everybody could smell it. It was bad. The kids started laughing, covering their mouths with their hands. The parents pretended not to notice, but they took to smiling. The ranger was caught in the act, and the only thing he could do was apologize to the group. He told them he was very sorry and didn't mean to do it.

The smell was such that the ranger cut short his talk about the fort's history and suggested the family look around the fort ruins, inside and out. They went outside, not surprisingly. A short time later they got in their car and left.

Seeing the car leave, the ranger was much relieved to know that the only witnesses to the incident were now gone. Only he knew about the fart as he waved his arms and hands around inside the museum, trying to chase away the smell.

He knew full well, however, that he had given that family a lifetime memory. Never would they forget about the ranger who farted, and they would be telling that story and laughing to countless people in the future.

Florida Summer - Part 1

After graduating from high school, I decided to go to Florida for the summer. I knew someone living near Key West and he invited me to visit. A friend of mine named Ted went with me. We packed our things in an old van that I had purchased for the trip. Before leaving we made a bunch of baloney sandwiches and put them in an ice chest. Mom told us not to put mayonnaise on the sandwiches because mayonnaise will spoil if it warms up. Ted and I didn't listen and we put butter and mayonnaise on quite a few sandwiches.

We started our drive from Iowa and it was several hundred miles before we checked our stash of food. There were only a few sandwiches left in the cooler. Mom had gotten into that cooler and took out 90 percent of our mayonnaise sandwiches. I was mad, so mad that somewhere along that trip I wrote her a letter expressing my opinion about her robbing sandwiches from our cooler.

Later I calmed down because it was obvious why she had done it. Spoiled mayonnaise is bad for the health. She worried about us getting sick, or worse.

When we reached Florida, we paid a visit to a college classmate of my sister, Janet. This young lady had a father who was a pilot in one of the wars. He loved to fly so he offered us a plane ride. We drove to a private airport and saw a beautiful P51 Mustang fighter plane sitting on the tarmac. There were numerous other planes parked around the airport, but all eyes were drawn to just one. It was showcase. This Mustang was polished yellow and ready for action. It was a two-seater, so maybe a trainer.

Both Ted and I got a ride. It flew so smoothly and easily. I'm usually prone to motion sickness but I did fine when this guy turned flips and loops. From my rear seat I was patting his shoulder.

Then it was back to our trip south. When our van finally reached the lower Florida Keys, we located the fellow who had invited me. He asked how long we intended to stay and we said all summer. This didn't please him; he expected us to stay a week. But he didn't say no so we hung around the marina all summer where he was staying. We slept in my van and ate peanut butter and jelly sandwiches. It became apparent that with little money to spend, our food intake would have to be spartan. So we ate peanut butter and jelly sandwiches for breakfast, noon, and evening meals along with water. What a diet. The only reason we survived that menu was because we were young and strong back then.

Maybe a couple of times each week, when the marina headquarters was empty of people, the owners would fumigate the inside for mosquitoes. During those spray sessions, which lasted 5-10 minutes, Ted would sometimes sneak inside and steal some candy bars to supplement his peanut butter and jelly diet.

Florida Summer - Part 2

My friend Ted and I did some skin diving during our summer trip to the Florida Keys. About every third day we would drive a short distance along the coast, pick a spot we liked, and then swim out in the ocean with masks, fins, and snorkels. The Atlantic coastal waters are warm, unlike the Pacific Coast. We would pull a small air-filled rubber raft behind us, which held our food, water, spear guns, and whatever else.

Our free diving was done in 5-15 feet of water, and we would swim around for several hours. The raft we would tether to vegetation on the bottom. Snorkeling like this for hours toughened us up and we got better at holding our breath.

One day I was snorkeling near some vegetation in ten feet of water and a large fish came over to check me out. I shot it with my spear gun and it suddenly ballooned into a pufferfish (inedible). Blood spewed everywhere as I tried to pull my spear tip from the fish. When I looked up, there in front of me about twenty feet away was a six-foot bull shark. This wasn't good.

I'm surrounded by blood so I instinctively glanced all around me to see if there were any other sharks lurking. There were not, so I waved my arm and spear gun at the shark to scare it away. The shark made a quick side turn and then glided slowly off, still watching me.

I hustled to push the spear point through the pufferfish and then unscrewed the tip from the shaft. Then I grabbed the speargun, shaft, and tip and quickly swam away from the bloody pufferfish. Awhile later I cautiously swam back to that area out of curiosity, and there on the sea floor was half a pufferfish.

One other diving excursion that Ted and I undertook turned out memorable. In fact, I still have regrets about that dive. We paddled offshore to an area that looked good. The bottom had vegetation and there were some angled slopes so we tied our raft over it. While swimming around the area, we noticed a long wooden plank on the bottom. Upon closer inspection, it turned out to be the bottom keel of a wooden ship. The ship was upside down under the sand with only about fifteen feet of the keel beam visible. There were pieces of wood and nails in the area. Some broken dishes were made of plastic, and from the look of the plastic, I guessed the ship to be 1800s. Ted and I paddled around and inspected the area for several hours looking for anything of value. No silver or gold coins were visible. Scattered here and there were piles of round rocks about the size of grapefruits.

Before leaving we attempted to triangulate the keel beam's location so we could find it again. There weren't many good triangulation objects along the shoreline, however, so we ended up just estimating distances in different directions. We were maybe a quarter mile from shore.

After driving back to the marina where we were staying, we told the owners and my friend about the shipwreck. Nobody paid much attention until we mentioned the piles of rock around the wreck site. It turned out that the piles of rock were ballast stone from the bottom of the ship. Ballast stones indicate an old ship. That meant our ship may have been 1700s.

My friend at the marina wanted to see the site so a couple of days later we loaded into his boat. We headed down the coast maybe a half mile. Then Ted and I began guesstimating distances and triangulating. When we got close, we jumped in the water and searched the area but no luck. We were unable to relocate that shipwreck.

If Ted and I had realized that this sunken ship might be old and have value, I'm sure we could have done better at triangulating that position. We were told by the marina owners that there are still known wrecks of value in that coastal area which haven't yet been found. To this day I'm still disappointed we could not relocate that wreck site. It would have been nice to let the marina owners know the exact location in case they wanted to investigate further.

I kept a souvenir from that shipwreck for many years. It was a long six-inch nail with a round head and flat hammered point. I still wonder how old that nail and ship were.

Florida Summer - Part 3

My Florida summer trip finally came to an end. My friend Ted and I had to return to Iowa for the start of school. We gathered our belongings, readied the van, and then had one more thing to do. We needed to steal a conch shell.

There was a motel with a swimming pool not far from where we were staying in the Florida Keys. Ted and I sometimes went there to hang out around the pool: swimming, diving, and checking out the females. Inside the office of the motel was a coffee table with a large polished conch shell on it. The shell was filled with paper match books and it was pretty. We wanted that conch shell.

We drove to the motel and parked the van. It was morning daylight hours. I was the getaway driver with the car engine running. Ted went inside and soon enough, here he came running. Match books were spilling out of the shell as he ran. I opened the passenger door, he jumped in, and off we went. I put the pedal down and kept a close eye on the rearview mirror. No police showed up so we got away clean.

Driving north up the Florida Coast highway seemed like forever. Finally we crossed into Georgia. One of us was driving at night and the other sleeping when there came a bang from the engine. It woke us up and we looked at each other. Maybe a minute later came another louder bang and the engine quit. We coasted onto the shoulder of the highway and parked. Looking at the engine, we saw that it had swallowed a valve. That engine was finished. We were halfway home.

The next morning we flagged down a motorist who phoned for help. A highway patrolman showed up and we had our van towed to nearby Cordele, Georgia. The patrolman lived there so we towed the van to his place. I told him he could keep the van and I would send him the title when I got back home, which I did.

The patrolman had a son a couple of years younger than Ted and I. He brought over some of his high school friends to check out the stuff in the van we needed to get rid of. We sold some things cheap and gave away the rest.

That evening Ted and I ate at the patrolman's home and we then went to town with his son and friends. They scooped the city streets in their cars and gathered at burger joints like we did back in Iowa. There was no mingling of whites with Blacks. It was all white groups of people here and Black groups of people there. Wherever our white group went, they were constantly bad-mouthing the Blacks. Driving around town, the whites would hurl insults at the Blacks. The Blacks didn't like it, but they didn't shout back. Clearly the whites didn't like the Blacks, and the Blacks didn't like the whites.

The next day Ted and I boarded a bus for Iowa with our luggage packed in boxes. Ted still had his conch shell. Ten years later I was living and traveling in a motorhome and I visited Ted in Arkansas. There in his living room was the conch shell. He was married at that time. He told me not to tell his wife how he got it; he had told her we found it while diving in deep water off the Florida Coast.

By the year 2000 I was in central California working as a federal park ranger. Another ranger whom I knew transferred to a ranger position in Georgia. He then returned a year later. I asked him how he liked rangering in Georgia. He said "no"; the people there were still fighting the Civil War. And I knew just what he meant. That's exactly what I saw in the late 1960s when I passed through southern Georgia.

Painting Water Towers

In the mid 1970s I was living and traveling in a motorhome. I didn't have much money so I asked about working on a crew that was painting a water tower in Arkansas. The boss said okay. The pay was low and help was hard to find. He started me out on the ground. A week later I was climbing the tower ladder.

One day the boss had gone somewhere and the work shift ended. I was on the tower catwalk with another worker. He got into the lift cage for a ride down. He signaled the lift operator on the ground to lower him down, but the cage was stuck and wouldn't move. He reached up and took hold of the metal catwalk above him and shook the cage. Suddenly the cage dropped a foot or two. The guy looked at his hand and then yelled to the ground operator to take him down fast. He was hurt.

I climbed down the ladder and locked up the company truck and trailer while the other two fellows headed to a hospital. The next morning everybody showed up for work. The injured worker had his hand wrapped, missing a finger. A worker climbed the tower ladder to the catwalk and pulled out a finger. The doctor at the hospital said he might have been able to reattach the finger if they had brought it with them the day before.

A couple of weeks later I was learning how to weld on the inside of a water tower tank. The seams inside needed rewelding. There was a small metal plate removed on the inside and I had to pee. Rather than pee inside the tank down the shaft, I aimed it out through the hole. Next we hear the boss on the ground yelling about the stream of water coming out of the tower. "What is that?" he wanted to know. I yelled down that I was peeing and he yelled up, "No Can Do!" He said that our company could lose the job and get in trouble with the Health Department. After that we had to climb down the ladder to pee or carry a bottle.

Next I graduated to scraping and painting the outside of the water towers. Starting at the top and working down, we would scrape rusty spots rather quickly. To get the underneath, we would hang from the catwalk on rope seats, swinging back and forth. After the scraping was done, it was time to take off my soft contact lenses and put on my thick glasses.

A large vat of water-based silver paint was mixed on the ground with a pressure pump hooked to it. One or two people on the ground would oversee the paint and pump and also look for spots that the painters missed. One or two painters would then start at the top and spray everything in sight. We would work our way down, swinging like monkeys under the tank. Last, we sprayed the legs. The painting took a couple of days to finish.

Painters always ended up covered in paint. It took a while to wash the paint off the skin. The clothes we took to the laundry.

After three months of doing several water-tower jobs in different cities, the spring weather began to warm. The boss got a call from home base in Michigan or Wisconsin. It was time to head back north where there was more contract money. Boss man asked me if I wanted to go north with them because I was a good painter. I said "No thanks."

Keith – The Drug Smuggler

I worked on riverboats in the late 1970s. When off the boats, I traveled around the U.S. in a motorhome. One trip took me to the Florida Panhandle where I decided to park alongside the Gulf of Mexico. I had no schedule and was doing some writing so I stayed there a week.

I was parked adjacent to a primary north/south highway. After a few days of not moving my vehicle, I began to notice unusual activity. Daily a dark green helicopter would fly over, sometimes more than once. Then a Coast Guard vessel began patrolling the Gulf waters offshore. I could see this from inside my RV (recreation vehicle).

Next came a group of adults doing a beach get-together on blankets between me and the shoreline, having a picnic on the sand. I decided there must be police involvement here; they must suspect me of being a drug courier for boats coming across the Gulf waters. I decided to leave.

I fired up my engine and drove down a frontage road toward the main highway. A man jogging toward me waved as I went by. I pulled onto the highway and just a short way down the road was the same jogger. He had pulled his car off the road and was waving at me to stop.

I pulled over and opened my door but all he had to say was small talk, which meant nothing. Then he asked if I would have sex with him. Now this is strange; doesn't happen every day. I told him no, closed my door, and drove on down the road heading south. It took me a while to figure out what that guy was up to.

I didn't drive far, maybe thirty miles, and found another quiet spot near the highway to park. Maybe 5-10 minutes later, I was sitting in the rear of my RV when I heard a noise. I looked up and a policeman had his nose pressed against my windshield. I got up, opened the door, and asked what he was doing. He said he was just checking around and making sure everything was okay.

I came to the conclusion that the police and Coast Guard were surveilling my RV in case I was involved with picking up drugs coming across the Gulf. The fellow who stopped me and asked if I would have sex with him must have been a cop looking for a way to arrest me and search my motorhome.

I decided enough was enough. By now these law enforcement people had become bothersome. I got a map and looked for a road heading east across the Panhandle. There was one nearby. That evening I headed out and took that road eastward toward the Atlantic coast for maybe fifty miles. Then I found a parking area beneath some large trees.

The next morning, sure enough, here comes the helicopter doing a flyover. It was the same chopper, but my RV wasn't visible overhead because of the trees. I waited a couple of hours and then drove east to the Florida coast. From there, instead of turning south, which was my original destination, I turned north along the coast.

I didn't have any more issues with police after that. I had lost them.

Texas Drilling Rig - Part 1

After graduating from college in 1971, I decided to take a winter drive south from Iowa. I gathered some belongings in my car and ended up in the southern tip of Texas near Kingsville. I lived in my car while looking for a job, but the only thing I could find was work on a land drilling rig. There was much oil drilling going on in that area of Texas so I asked around and got a job on a rig that was drilling for oil on the King Ranch.

I found a cheap apartment not far away and began moving in. In the living room, which was carpeted, I accidentally dropped a (hard) contact lens from my eye while removing it. Without contacts or glasses, I'm legally blind so it was imperative that I find that lens. My rig job was starting soon.

I've lost and searched for hard contact lenses before so I knew the routine. Without moving my feet, I scanned all of the floor around me. No contact lens. Then I carefully backed away, making sure not to step on anything. Getting down on my knees, I scoured the carpet in all directions. I could see no lens. Next I carefully searched around a couple of boxes on the floor where I had dropped the lens. I looked on top and inside the boxes but no luck. Time was passing and I was mad but there was no other option. I had to find that lens. I was getting worried.

Then I looked at the outside of the boxes and, believe it or not, there it was. Stuck on the vertical outside of the box was my contact lens. Somehow moisture on the lens had allowed it to stick to the outside vertical cardboard when I dropped it. It was undamaged.

I was greatly relieved and furious about this two-hour search. What were the odds of that contact lens falling and sticking to the outside of a box and the slim odds of me finding it there? I considered myself lucky. My life was back to normal.

Days later I was working on a land drilling rig. The rig worked all day, every day, and I was part of a five or six man shift. One day we were pulling all of the drill pipe out of the hole. We stacked the pipe in stands of three alongside the drill platform. Then we pulled the drill collar pipes, which are thicker and heavier. Last we pulled out a collar pipe attached to the drill bit which needed to be moved off the platform.

A huge hoist holding the collar pipe vertical was being operated by the toolpusher. The rest of our crew, including the driller, began to manually push the massive collar to the edge of the drill platform. I was in the middle of the group pushing. We pushed hard but the collar was too heavy. It got close to the edge but then stopped and began slowly swinging back. Everybody kept pushing against it, though, as the collar slowly swung back toward the pipe stand opposite the hole. Not until the last minute did the group break away from the push. I was boxed in the middle and couldn't get out as the swinging collar closed in on the stand pipe.

Just in time I managed to pull my leg from between the pipes, but my hard hat got caught. The two pipes began squeezing my hard hat, which was made of tough plastic, and I couldn't pull my head out. Suddenly my head popped backward, and the hard hat jetted out the other side of the pipes. My head was okay. My leg was okay. I was uninjured.

One of the workers jokingly said it was lucky that I was hard-headed. If my leg had been caught between the two pipes, it would have been crushed. If the top of my head had remained between the pipes, it would have been crushed. The hard hat saved my life. I felt very fortunate that evening going home alive and unhurt.

Texas Drilling Rig - Part 2

A toolpusher is a person who oversees all work being done on a land drilling rig. Usually the toolpusher is an old driller who lives in a trailer at the rig site. Workers on the drilling platform are called roughnecks. I was a new worker on the platform so I was called a worm.

One day I was toiling at some ground task near the drilling rig and the toolpusher walked up to me. He had a rig dog by his side and he handed me a (jalapeno pepper) wild berry. He had just picked it and said I should try it. Maybe I would like it. I looked at the small dark berry and put it into my mouth and bit down. Fire shot through my mouth as I spit it out. I looked around at the toolpusher who was walking away. Later he told some of the roughnecks that the new guy must be tough if he could eat wild jalapenos. He didn't see me spit it out.

During the oil-drilling process, when the liquid mud begins to show oil, a blowout preventer is set over the hole. Our crew driller was named Buddy, and he and I became friends. We were screwing large lug nuts onto bolts atop the blowout preventer, making sure the bolts were lubed and threaded properly. The top hole was supposed to be covered but Buddy and I didn't bother with the cover. Then I accidentally dropped a lug nut into the hole. "Oops" was all I could say, and Buddy knew there was nothing we could do about it. That lug nut was headed to the bottom of the hole, and it was a big nut made of steel. Buddy put a cover over the hole and we finished the lug nut job.

A day or two later the drill bit stopped making downward progress so we had to pull all of the pipe out of the hole to see why. One of the three diamond-tipped rotors on the bottom of the drill bit was broken off. Gee, I wonder why? I hadn't said anything to anyone about dropping a big lug nut into the hole, and I'm quite sure Buddy didn't either.

Our crew spent the next week fishing for steel parts at the bottom of the hole. There is a tool gadget designed for this purpose. Finally we pulled some metal from the hole and started drilling for oil again. I knew I had set the drilling schedule back a week and Buddy did too, but we never said anything. The toolpusher would not have been pleased.

I worked that rig job until Spring and then decided to go back home. Before I left for Iowa, Buddy told me a story about himself. He had a wife and family and had been an alcoholic. He tried treatment for his addiction to alcohol. One night while going to sleep he was pleading to God and himself about fixing his drinking problem. Finally he drifted into sleep and then something happened: he said he took a trip. He consciously ended up somewhere apart from his physical body. He didn't say what his surroundings looked like or if he saw or talked to anyone. Sometime later in the night he found himself back inside his physical body again.

He was so moved by this experience that he wanted to tell other people that there is life after death. He promptly went out and bought a large evangelist tent so he could invite people to come and listen to his story. He had a new mission in life. But as the days passed, he slowly began to lose his nerve about public speaking. He told me his new evangelist tent still sat unused in his garage.

At that time I wasn't a believer in anything paranormal, so I didn't give much credence to Buddy's story. Good for him if it helped him, but I passed it off as a vivid dream. Five years later I was trying meditation when I learned about out-of-the-body travel. After I had some conscious out-of-body experiences of my own, I was better able to appreciate Buddy's story.

Custer's Last Stand

Back in 1979 I spent some time in southern Montana fishing for trout. I was living in a motorhome then and had no schedule. I met an elderly couple and they introduced me to their friend, Bill. Bill was visiting them and he had driven all the way from Maryland to hunt for war artifacts on the Little Bighorn Battlefield. Bill was a George Custer enthusiast and a member of a Custer organization that met yearly in the north central states. Members like Bill knew much about General George Custer and the Battle of the Little Bighorn which happened in 1876 in south central Montana.

For this trip Bill was traveling and living in a pickup camper. He invited me to do some metal detecting with him on the Custer battlefield so I accepted. The next day we drove to the Little Bighorn National Battlefield Monument which wasn't far away. Bill knew the area and parked in a secluded spot. We climbed the boundary fence to get off park property and walked around for several hours with metal detectors. Bill had brought an extra metal detector. We dug up lead bullets and cartridge shells and then headed back to his elderly friends' home.

The following morning we did the same thing, but this time we took a roll of twine. When we found an area that had metal artifacts, we put down a string line and walked the string line. Bill's detector reached down twelve inches and mine only detected to six inches so he found twice as many relics as I did. That day we found about thirty bullets and cartridge cases which pleased him.

After driving back home, we looked over the finds. There were 58 caliber lead bullets and shell casings which the soldiers had fired. All of the soldiers were carrying a single-shot 58 caliber rifle. We also had lead bullets and shell casings from smaller caliber guns like the Henry and Spencer rifles used by the Indians. This meant that soldiers and Indians were shooting at each other in close proximity.

One particular 58 caliber cartridge shell that I found looked different from the others. Bill recognized it as a brass cartridge shell and not copper. He said all the soldiers fired copper cartridge shells, and the only officer in Custer's command who fired brass shells that he knew of was General George Custer. Custer may have fired that bullet himself.

The next day Bill and I made another trip to the battlefield. A friend of his who lived in the area drove out to join us. Bill parked in a secluded place, but when this guy arrived, he parked in a visible spot near the fence where we were digging. A park ranger soon drove up and yelled over the fence that we couldn't metal detect there. He said we would have to leave. I asked the ranger if he had any authority on the Indian reservation land where we were metal detecting. He said no and then got in his pickup and left. We didn't see him again.

After a half day of walking and digging, Bill and I said good bye to his friend and we headed home. By now I'd seen the ground layout around the battlefield. Bill and I looked at his map of the battle site showing the Sioux and Cheyenne Indian village on the west side of the Little Bighorn River. He showed me where Captain Benteen and Major Reno had taken six companies of soldiers, as directed by Custer, to strike the south end of the village. All of those troops were soon driven back by Indian fire to a high-ground defensive position east of the river. Reno and Benteen could hear Custer's men shooting, but they couldn't ride to help. They remained pinned down for another day and a half.

Testimony came later from Reno's and Benteen's soldiers that there were some white buffalo hunters among the Indians during the fight. One soldier witnessed a white marksman with a powerful buffalo gun shoot two soldiers beside him from long distance. Bill told me there were perhaps half a dozen whites living with and fighting alongside the Indians.

What isn't clear about the Battle of the Little Bighorn is what Custer did after Reno and Benteen left him. Custer had five companies of troops, about 210 men, and he rode toward the north end of the Indian village. Halfway there, Custer stopped and did two things. He sent a rider message back to Reno and Benteen telling them to join him and bring packs. He also split his forces. Two companies of troops rode west toward the center of the village, and the other three companies headed toward the north end of the Indian camp. Historians believe Custer went with the two companies of troops riding west toward the center of the village.

All this time Custer made the assumption that he had surprised the enemy and the Indians would flee when attacked. Neither was true. The Indians knew Custer was coming and they were ready and willing to fight. Indians outnumbered soldiers by four to one and some of them had rifles.

What happened after Custer's five companies were divided was that both groups were soon in full retreat. They located each other in the melee from the sound of gunshots, and all died in the same general area. The battleground is open terrain with some gullies and slopes but not many bushes, shrubs, or trees. A final desperate escape attempt was made on foot by the last fifty soldiers, including Custer, but that ended at the Last Stand which is just a dirt hill. The horses were all dead so the men didn't get far.

As I listened to Bill's story and looked at the map, I offered him a different battle theory. My guess was that Custer would have stayed with the larger group of soldiers riding to the north end of the village. As that group neared the river, gunshots from the trees there forced the three companies back. The two companies making a center attack on the village met the same resistance at the river and retreated back the way they came from. All five companies found each other in the chaos by following the gunfire, and they all died in the same area.

Bill thought my battle plan had merit. He had heard about a skirmish line of bullets and cartridges being found years ago by metal detectors, located just east of the river and north of the village. Historians have assumed that the three companies of soldiers riding north didn't go past the Last Stand area. My belief was that this group of soldiers was led by Custer, and they did ride to the river where they met gunfire. They then fell back to the battlefield area, which is where the other two retreating soldier companies joined them. Bill said he would offer up this battle theory at his next Custer convention.

Bill and I kept in touch after he left. We would meet again.

Death at Kaweah

My first year working at Lake Kaweah, near Visalia in central California, saw twelve deaths at the park. I was a new park ranger there and had no experience as a law enforcement ranger. It was "learn on the job" and Kaweah is an active lake. Initially I was given a warning pad to write warnings only. Not until months later did I get further training, which included a citation book for writing tickets to violators. Corps of Engineers park rangers don't carry guns so serious park problems and violations require a call to the police.

That year of 1991/92 there were seven traffic fatalities on the road passing by the lake. There was one diving death, three drownings, and one suicide. The suicide occurred at the marina parking lot during the hot summer. I checked on a report of a body in a car and found a young Asian male in the driver's seat of his car. He had been there overnight and the heat had turned his skin almost black. I called for a sheriff deputy who came and handled the case. The young man had taken pills to end his life. I wrote an incident report for the park.

One of the drownings happened at the upper end of the lake where the Kaweah river flows in. An elderly man, his wife, and their young son were on a rented houseboat. A fishing line got caught on the shore so the man tried to swim a short distance to the bank to unhook it. He couldn't swim and drowned. When I got to the scene, the sheriff dive team had just arrived. They suited up and went down and paddled around for more than thirty minutes before surfacing and announcing they had located the body. The deputy on scene was irritated because he told them where the body would be found. The water was clear and only 15-20 feet deep. So why did it take so long to find the body?

I thought about this question and could only come up with three reasons. One, the dive team may have purposely paddled around awhile to accumulate more dive time and thus reap more dive pay. Two, the dive team may have waited awhile so they wouldn't have to do CPR on the body after recovery. Three, both of the above.

It was repulsive for me to think about what this dive team had done and not done. But there's no question they could have dove to the bottom in clear water and pulled that body up in five minutes' time.

My second year at Lake Kaweah saw one or two deaths. Occasionally we had a drowning or some other accident. The death rate for Kaweah after my first year was about 1 ½ deaths per year. The death rate for other Corps of Engineers lakes in California is between zero and one per year.

William Shatner

In the mid 1990s I was a park ranger working at Lake Kaweah in central California. Occasionally we would see William Shatner, the famous Star Trek commander, at the lake. He worked in Los Angeles and had a vacation home northeast of Lake Kaweah.

Shatner and some friends of his were rafting down the Kaweah River one spring when they came upon a river rescue scene. A raft had overturned and some people were hanging on to island trees. The river current was fairly strong and the water level was up. A sheriff deputy from the nearby town of Three Rivers was on scene and Shatner helped him get a rope to the people in need of help. The stranded people were pulled to safety and no one was hurt. The overturned raft was recovered and Shatner's group continued rafting downriver to Lake Kaweah.

I heard about this incident a few days later from the deputy who was involved with the rescue. Several weeks later I was patrolling the upper end of Lake Kaweah and saw the Three Rivers raft company there. I stopped for a chat and they pointed to Shatner's group pulling off the river below us. Shatner and a lady plus another family of four carried their two rafts up to the parking lot for transport back to Three Rivers. I went over and asked William if his television producers were going to include his river rescue in their Rescue 911 television series, which he was starring in then. He said they were considering it.

I don't think that ever happened. I don't recall any television Rescue 911 episode having a river rescue theme.

Robbers

I was about thirty years of age, parked for the night in my motorhome which I was living in then. I don't remember which state I was in, somewhere southeast, but I was parked in an isolated parking area that had blacktop and one overhead light. I was doing dishes in the evening when another car pulled into the parking area. The vehicle did a slow wide circle and then pulled close alongside my RV and stopped. My window curtains were open so I could see the car outside in the dim light. I dried my hands and opened my door but the car was too close.

I still remember what I said to the driver whom I couldn't see very well. I said "What's the deal fellas? You're parked so close to me I can't open up my f-cking door." The driver then asked if I knew the way out. His voice sounded like a young guy about twenty-five years old. Another fellow in the passenger seat said something to him in a low voice. I told the driver that the way out was the same way he came in. He said okay and then slowly drove forward. The car went slowly out the way it came in. At the entrance, the car turned right onto a main roadway and began speeding up.

I watched through my window as the car drove off. It was a large, older, dark-colored vehicle with wing taillights. As the taillights disappeared over a hill, I began to realize what this was all about. Those two fellows saw my RV in an isolated area and were thinking about robbing me. There was no other explanation for what they did. They pulled alongside my motorhome to look inside and see who was there. Maybe an easy victim?

I grabbed my rifle, made sure it had ammunition, went outside and locked my RV door. Then I waited in some nearby bushes in the dark for ten minutes to see if they were desperate enough to come back. They did not.

End of story? Not quite.

When I went back inside my motorhome to finish my dishes, a car horn began blaring not far away. That car horn blasted for about fifteen minutes before it finally stopped. Nothing more happened that evening or night.

The next morning I got up and prepared to drive on, but out of curiosity I decided to drive up a road in the direction of the horn noise I'd heard the previous evening. Not far up that road I passed a small house that was burned to the ground. Ashes were still smoking as two fire marshals walked around looking for a source of fire. No walls were left standing. It was obvious that the horn I heard the evening before was someone blowing a car horn to wake any occupants inside.

I felt sure that my visitors the previous evening had something to do with this fire. They drove off just before the horn sounded. I hadn't realized it at the time, but the previous evening when I spoke to the driver in a confrontational manner, that must have given them pause about committing any mischief. Maybe this guy wouldn't be an easy takedown. They decided to move on.

Zip Line

I was staying on Fremont Street in Las Vegas with a lady friend for a few days. Fremont Street is old-town Las Vegas with lots of people, casinos, and crazy sights to see. It's a "must see" for everybody. An overhead electric light display stretches for two blocks and puts on amazing shows every hour on the hour after 8 PM. Multiple outdoor bands are playing in the evening, and there's an overhead zip line for visitors to ride. Tourist groups walk Fremont Street at night just to see the lights and sights.

I had been to Fremont Street numerous times before and watched people ride the zip line. On this trip I started thinking about doing it as a new experience. The lady I was with was several years older than me and I was retired so we weren't young. She wasn't in prime shape and was carrying some extra weight, so I knew what she would say if I suggested we ride the zip line.

It was St. Patrick's week and I had on a tall white and green stove pipe hat. My lady friend was wearing a green wig. I suggested we walk to where the zip line started, so we did. At the base of the zip line we looked around and saw the ticket booth. I went over and asked about the cost of a zip ride and was told $20. I said I wanted two tickets, paid the fee, and presented one to my lady friend. She looked at the ticket and took it only because it was already paid for and she didn't want to say no and disappoint me.

We walked up three flights of stairs where we got harnessed and placed in line. She was nervous but putting on a smiley face, hanging in as best she could. Five minutes later we were standing side by side at the tower opening looking down. A safety crew hooked us up to the zip line and I jumped first. I was zipping along, looking down at people who were looking up at me. My tall hat I was holding on my head to keep it from flying off. I looked back and here comes my lady friend. She's zipping. Her body is flattened out, legs forward, one hand holding her green wig on her head. The wire cable above us is singing away as we zip toward the landing zone halfway down Fremont Street. I look down again at the people below who are looking up at me. It's fun, but it doesn't last very long.

Thirty seconds later I begin to slow down and come to a halt. I look behind me and my lady friend is approaching the landing with a big smile on her face. She reaches the end as I'm standing up and tells me how great and exciting that was. She's ready to go again.

Manager Joe

When I began working at Fort Selden State Monument as a park ranger in the late 1980s, Joe was manager there. Fort Selden in southern New Mexico has low visitation so we only had two permanent rangers plus Manager Joe. The fort is open seven days a week.

Joe was about thirty years of age with a wife and kids. He was new to managing and he had bad breath. You could smell his breath across a room. Why his wife and kids didn't tell him about his bad breath is a mystery. One day after he had eaten lunch, I decided to give him a hint. From across the room I asked him if he had onions with his meal. Sitting twenty feet away, he looked at me and said, "No. Why did I ask?" I told him his breath smelled like onions.

Several days later Joe came to work and reported that he'd been to a dentist and discovered he had severe gingivitis. I'm guessing he asked his wife about his breath and decided to see a dentist. The dentist told him that his gingivitis was so advanced that he might lose all of his teeth. Weeks passed and with the dentist's help, Joe was able to cure his gingivitis and save his teeth.

Joe told me stories about a park ranger who had worked for him at Fort Selden before I arrived. Joe said he caught the fellow red-handed stealing money. He had set a money trap and the guy failed the test. Joe had taken management training and learned some tricks about checking the honesty of employees. For me this was a red flag; he would do the same to me. The amazing thing was that he was telling me this. Not the smartest guy in the world.

Some weeks later it was closing time at the fort but there were people still looking around. I told Joe I would stay and he could go. I was out front with the visitors when I saw him exit the museum and walk to his car. More visitors showed up so I went into the museum with them. I looked at the donation jar and it now had a $20 dollar bill in it. That bill wasn't there earlier and I knew immediately where it came from. Joe was testing me.

Fifteen minutes later, I was still in the museum with a family when Joe returned. I knew why he was back. He walked in, looked around for a few minutes, and then left. He thought I would be gone by then and was checking on his $20 bill.

When the visitors finally left, I locked up and went home. The next day I went to work as usual. There was Joe and there was his $20 dollar bill in the donation jar. He never said anything about it.

After that episode I began checking on employment with the federal government. I had to take some written tests to qualify, which I did, and that put my name on a federal hiring list. Following that came a phone call from Lake Kaweah in California about a park ranger opening there. I said "yes" to that and "so long" to Manager Joe.

Billy the Kid

Years ago I worked at Fort Sumner State Monument in New Mexico where Billy the Kid was killed. During my two years there, I fielded a lot of questions about the Kid.

Much of Billy's background is murky. He told friends he came from New York City so it's believed he was born there between the years 1859-1861. His mother, Catherine McCarty, moved west seeking warmer climate for her declining health. In 1873 she relocated her family to Silver City, New Mexico, where she died the following year from tuberculosis.

Did Billy graduate to robbing banks and trains? No. Billy's thefts involved food, cattle, and horses. He stole to survive and never had much money.

Was Billy a handsome ladies' man? No. Billy was small frame and had buck teeth. But he was friendly and people liked him.

Was Billy a marksman and quick on the draw? Apparently yes. He did practice quick-drawing but never got into a quick-draw shootout. He did a lot of target practice so he became a proficient marksman.

Was he right- or left-handed? An early tin-type photo shows Billy with a pistol and holster on his left hip. That photo is a reverse image. Early movies have Billy as a lefty but he was right-handed.

How many men did Billy kill? From history that I've read, Billy was involved in the killing of 11 men. Four were killed by Billy alone. The other seven were killed by Billy together with his outlaw friends. This means that bullets from Billy's gun probably killed about seven or eight men.

In 1881 Billy escaped jail in Lincoln, New Mexico, after killing two deputies. Sheriff Pat Garrett went looking for him in Fort Sumner not far away. At night Garrett visited Pete Maxwell in his bedroom and asked the whereabouts of the Kid. Just then Billy entered Pete's room and spoke. Garrett knew Billy's voice but couldn't see if Billy had a gun so he fired. Billy was unarmed.

The small cemetery where Billy is now buried is adjacent to Fort Sumner State Monument. Billy is buried next to two of his outlaw pals. Years ago some of the headstones in that cemetery were knocked around and moved by heavy equipment so Billy and others buried there may not rest exactly where they are now marked. But their skeletal remains should be close by.

Could Billy's skeleton be identified today if it was dug up? Probably yes, for two reasons. Billy had buck teeth, and those teeth would be intact today. Also, his body was dressed by Deluvina Maxwell who was part of the Maxwell family. She put an oversized white shirt on Billy's body to make him look proper for burial. The back of that shirt was tucked and pinned with a large metal safety pin. If that pin hasn't rusted away, it can identify Billy's skeleton.

How many "the Kids" were there in the Wild West during Billy's time? I know of four, and none of them were called "Billy the Kid." Only the newspapers, comic books, books, and movies used the name Billy the Kid. They were all called "the Kid." There was one Kid in the Panhandle of western Oklahoma. Another spent time in the Santa Fe jail. There was William Bonney who we know today as "Billy the Kid." Also, Billy Clanton in Tombstone, Arizona, who died in a gunfight at the OK Corral in 1881.

What about Brushy Bill Roberts from Hico, Texas, who later claimed to be William Bonney, the real Billy the Kid? About 1907 was when Ollie Roberts began suffering from mental delusions. His mental disorder may have advanced to where he actually believed he was Billy the Kid. He was not. He passed away in 1950 still claiming to be Billy the Kid.

Canada

I got off a work boat in St. Paul, Minnesota, in the mid 1970s and decided to see Canada. Why not? I'd never been there. I had a motorhome and no schedule so I started driving. After crossing the border into Manitoba, I turned east through Ontario. Next came Quebec with French-speaking citizens. Then I took a ferry ride to New Brunswick. From there I aimed southward through the New England states. It was Fall then and the leaves were beautiful. In New York state I stopped off at Niagara Falls for a look-see. Then I drove back to St. Paul for another month of work on a riverboat.

The following year I saw some sights in western Canada. In Alberta Province I drove up the scenic highway through Banff and Jasper National Parks. In Manitoba I met a family and parked my RV at their place for several weeks. The father, his son, and some friends took me on several pack trips into the bush to camp overnight and fish the lakes. They knew the area, and they also knew an inexpensive flying service. For a cheap fee the flying service flew us to a lake with an island. The plane landed on water and left us on the island which had a boat, motor, and gasoline for us to use. We camped there and fished for northern pike and walleye for several days. I caught a fifteen-pound northern pike. Then the plane returned and flew us home.

That bush trip prompted me to call a friend back in Iowa. I told him to come to Manitoba and we could do some cheap fly-in fishing. He said fine and showed up days later. He and I flew in and fished for several days. We slept in a tent, cooked fish that we caught, and also fought off mosquitoes, ticks, and flies constantly. The insects and bugs in the north woods are bad.

The following year I made it to British Columbia on the west coast by way of Seattle. I drove my motorhome onto a ferry and floated to Vancouver. After visiting Butchart Gardens, I drove eastward into gold country. People told me about miners working gold claims back in "them thar hills." I decided to try my hand at panning for gold so I went to a store and bought what I needed. I built a small sluice box with wooden riffles and headed out to the gold claims. I drove down a crooked road to a miner's plot that had a swift stream running through it. The miner was alone and I introduced myself. He looked me over and could tell that I wouldn't be carrying away much of his gold using my Mickey Mouse equipment so he gave me the okay. We became friends.

I stayed about a week on his claim and it was mercifully hard work. I set my small sluice box in the stream rapids and then poured dirt, sand, and gravel into it. The coarse rock I pushed through the box by hand to clear the waste. The black sand and gold flakes settled in the bottom of the sluice box behind the wooden riffles. The dirt, sand, and gravel that I dug came from the stream at bedrock level, which was inches below the water. Placer gold is moved by water and rests on bedrock so the dirt and sand that I wanted for my sluice was just above bedrock. I would fill two buckets, carry them to the sluice and pour them in, doing this over and over for hours. Talk about hard labor. Why was I doing this?

When the sluice box got full of black sand, I would pick it up and empty it into a large plastic garbage can that I brought. Then I would reset the sluice box in fast water. The last step to getting gold was panning the black sand by hand with a gold pan. The flakes of gold shine brightly as the black sand is carefully washed out of the pan.

I kept my gold in a small glass bottle. The flakes were tiny except for two nuggets that had some size. After a week of this my groceries ran out, which meant it was time to go. I had seen and done enough placer gold mining. My week's profit was less than $50 worth of loose gold and it was very hard work. I now had more respect for miners and what they do. I gave my equipment to the miner except for my gold pan which I kept. I wrote letters to him for several years afterward.

From the British Columbia gold fields, I headed back to the States. I drove through a large city in Montana, probably Butte, and saw a mining museum there so I stopped. After looking around inside the museum, I asked an attendant if they had need for a small amount of placer gold. He was interested and said they were considering putting out a display with gold in a gold pan. I got my small bottle with gold flakes plus another small bottle filled with black sand and donated them to the museum. Maybe that pan display is still there.

Near Drowning

Imagine yourself as a parent taking several of your children to a swim beach at Eastman Lake in California. You can't swim. Your children can't swim, and you have no life jackets. Your oldest daughter, age 16, brings an air mattress and fills it with air at the beach. She then gets on the mattress and paddles around in shallow water. There are no other people on the beach or in the area, just you and your kids. There is only one boater on the lake. He is fishing alone at the dam which is about 100 yards away.

Your daughter on the air mattress drifts perhaps 100 feet from shore and then slips off the mattress. A light breeze pushes the mattress out of her reach so now she's drowning in front of your eyes. She's flailing in the water and yelling for help because she can't swim. You can't swim. You can't help her. So what do you do? You yell for help to the only boater on the lake and hope he can hear you.

That boater did hear the cries for help that day and turned to see a man yelling and waving at him from the beach. Then he saw the air mattress and a person struggling in the water. He quickly reeled his fish line in, fired up his engine, and raced his boat to the drowning girl.

He told me later that she was lifeless when he grabbed her and pulled her into his boat. She was going under for the last time. She spit water for a while and had to rest and regain her strength, but she was alive. The boater retrieved the air mattress and delivered the girl to her father on the beach.

I heard about this incident several weeks after it happened, from that hero fisherman. I knew him; I was a park ranger at Eastman Lake. It made the fisherman feel good to know that he had actually saved a person's life.

My thoughts went to the father standing on the beach. Think of the range of emotions he went through watching his daughter nearly drown and then being saved.

St. Paul Harlem

I was in St. Paul, Minnesota, staying overnight in my motorhome in the parking lot of a shopping mall. Morning came and I was sitting at my table when a group of boys walked by. Through the curtains I could see about ten colored youths maybe 8-10 years old. A minute later came a loud bang against the front of my RV. I opened the front curtains to see the group looking at me. On the asphalt in front of my motorhome was a big rock.

I put my shoes on, opened the door, and raced after them. They scattered like flies. I aimed for three who were running together. Two of them peeled off, but I caught the middle kid and grabbed him by his neck. I started marching him back to my motorhome a block away.

As this was happening, motorists driving by were watching and wondering. Kids were running through the street, dodging traffic. Several cars pulled over and stopped, then several more. Black males were getting out of their cars and walking towards me. When I got to the parking lot with the kid in tow, about five Black males had me surrounded. They were barking at me about chasing kids into traffic and grabbing one of them. The boy I held was pleading that he didn't do it. The other boys threw the rock.

All I could do was point to the big rock in front of my RV and tell the men that the boys had thrown it. They looked over and saw the rock and heard what the boy was saying. They knew the rest of the story.

They told me to let the boy go. Then they told the boy not to throw rocks and go tell his friends not to throw rocks. I turned and walked back to my RV, and they went back to their cars. As I glanced around, it wasn't until then that I realized where I was. All the vehicles passing by were driven by Blacks. All the people walking in and out of the mall were Blacks. This was Colored Town. I was a white guy in Harlem.

Rita's Bird

Ron and Rita were campground hosts at Lake Kaweah in California when I joined the ranger staff there. One of the campers brought Rita a tiny sparrow that had fallen out of a nest. Rita tried to save the bird by putting it in a Kleenex box in the campground office and feeding it a mixture of milk and potatoes. The little bird didn't die; it kept getting a little bigger as the days passed. Rita called the bird Tweety and talked to it when she fed it. Gradually the bird began to recognize Rita's voice.

When the little sparrow began to show feathers, it started walking and hopping around the campground office. By then it recognized Rita as its mother so it would hop onto her finger, arm, or shoulder. When campers entered or exited the campground, they might see a sparrow perched on Rita's shoulder. When the bird's feathers grew large enough, Rita started giving flying lessons. She would set Tweety down somewhere, then move a few feet away and call for it. The little bird would lift and flap its wings and fly the short distance to Rita's arm or finger.

Tweety had become Rita's pet by now so she moved the sparrow into her trailer. The bird was learning to fly but she kept it indoors and fed it there. The sofa in Ron and Rita's trailer had some brown coloring, and one day Tweety sat on the sofa where the brown colors matched. Rita sat down on the sofa, not seeing Tweety there. That was the end of Tweety. When she discovered what had happened, Rita cried for two days. Ron took the bird outside and dug a hole in the ground for a proper burial. It took several weeks for Rita to get over the loss of her favorite little bird.

Desperado

After I retired, a lady friend and I took a trip to Las Vegas by way of Yosemite National Park. We packed our things plus two sleeping bags in the back of my Saturn station wagon and headed northeast from Clovis, California, to Yosemite. We drove through the park and then on to Bodie further north, which is an old abandoned mining town. From Bodie we went south to nearby Mono Lake, then dry camped that night in my car at Mammoth Lakes. The next day we drove around the Mammoth Lake area which is beautiful, a snow-skiing mecca in winter. Driving south from there, we went through the town of Bishop and then passed by Mt. Whitney on our way to Four Corners. We stayed the night in Primm, which is just inside Nevada on the road to Las Vegas.

That evening from an outside hot tub at Primm Valley Casino, my lady friend and I watched the Desperado outdoor train ride. It didn't look intimidating. The next day we went to where the train starts, inside Buffalo Bill's Casino, and presented our coupons for a free ride. An usher seated us side by side behind two kids, a brother and sister maybe nine and twelve years old. We asked them if the ride was scary and they said "no". This was their fourth ride that day. A loud speaker came on telling riders that old people shouldn't ride, people with high blood pressure shouldn't ride, and don't wear glasses during the ride. Then we got rolling.

The train creeped upward to a high point and then began coasting downhill. The two kids in front of us turned around with happy faces and told us we could start getting scared now. They were holding their hands high in the air, having a fun time. My lady friend and I started feeling the gravity forces. As the train banked right at high speed, I was holding on for dear life. The next couple of minutes passed by like a blur because they were a blur. I held a death grip through right turns and left turns, ups and downs, and this went on for a full two minutes. I was terrified.

Finally the train coasted to a stop. My head was throbbing. An usher came over to help us and my lady friend told her it was the worst ride of her life. She was holding her neck. I stood up and saw my sunglasses flattened on my seat. Somehow those sunglasses had traveled from my shirt pocket to beneath my buttocks. We both wobbled away and back to our room. I took a couple of Excedrin tablets and laid down in bed. My lady friend had pain in her neck and said she felt and heard something pop in her neck during the ride. She had pain in her neck for months afterward.

After a nap we felt a little better and went forth to the casinos to gamble away some of our money. As for the Desperado, that ride is built for and better suited for the younger generation. It visually resembles the train ride that circles around and through the New York New York Casino in Las Vegas.

The Roswell Incident

Bill and I agreed to meet near Roswell, New Mexico, at a certain date, time, and location. I knew Bill from years earlier when we metal detected for war artifacts near the Custer Battlefield in Montana. We kept in touch afterward, and he learned I was working as a park ranger at Fort Sumner in eastern New Mexico. Bill was interested in the Roswell Incident which occurred in 1947. A mysterious flying object crashed near Roswell, and a story of an alien spacecraft grew out of that incident. Bill wanted to see the crash site for himself.

He had driven from his home in Maryland to attend an annual gathering of Custer enthusiasts in Michigan or Wisconsin. Then he drove his pickup camper south to New Mexico to explore the Roswell Incident. I drove to meet him near Roswell and we headed out from there.

Bill knew approximately where the crash site was located so we drove to an urban area not far away and asked around. Only one lady knew anything about it. She knew a fellow living in the area who definitely knew where the crash site was. She warned us, however, that he would not tell us the location. She did give us directions to where he lived.

Outside of town we found the guy's home where he raised cattle. Bill and I stopped at the house and went to the door. He was home and we told him we were interested in the Roswell Incident. He let us inside and we all sat down in the living room. I told him that we knew he knew where the Roswell Incident happened and that we were willing to pay him to show us that location. He said he wouldn't show us the location, which he knew, but he would tell us the story.

When the accident happened back in 1947, he was living in the area. After hearing about it, he went to the crash site to have a look. He said the debris appeared a little strange, maybe a balloon of some kind but not an alien craft. Not much news came out at first until some high-ranking military personnel showed up for an inspection. Then the newspapers and television reporters became interested. They went to the crash site and interviewed anyone they could find, including the fellow telling this story. They asked if it could have been an alien craft and were there any aliens seen. He played along and said it might have been an alien craft because he had seen some small creatures scurrying around.

Now the news reporters were on to a hot story. Alien creatures had been spotted at the crash site near Roswell, New Mexico. Other news outlets now picked up on the story. When asked about the little creatures and what they looked like, he described them as small, running around, not human, and he managed to rope one of them. The little critter got away but now the story was growing. A cattle rancher had roped one of the small creatures so it must have happened. The rancher lived in the area and saw the debris field. He roped one of the aliens so it must be true. The guy was laughing as he told this story to Bill and me.

We talked awhile longer and the fellow wouldn't budge on showing us where the crash site was. Bill felt somewhat satisfied about the Roswell Incident mystery after listening to the rancher's story. He was disappointed that it wasn't a spacecraft.

My conclusion was that this is a classic example of how fake news is born. The Roswell Incident has become a famous story here in the U. S., told in many books and documentaries. Did the mystery craft come from Area 51? Did the military suppress information? If so, why?

Now when I see or hear something about the Roswell Incident, I pass it off. And if there's mention of possible aliens seen at the Roswell crash site, rest assured that is definitely not true. I talked to the fellow who fabricated that story.

Washington, D.C.

During the years when I was driving my motorhome around the U. S., I went up and down the East Coast a couple of times. I saw all the states from New England to Florida. I visited relatives in New England who took me to some of the Revolutionary War memorials. Aunt Ann and her husband, Herb, took me to Rhode Island for a boat ride. I saw the Fall colors in both New York state and New England twice. I drove through the freeway congestion of New York City and Philadelphia with white knuckles. I stopped at historic sites from New Jersey down through the Carolinas. I even went to Disney World and Sea World in Florida.

On one of those trips I visited Washington, D.C. There are a lifetime of museums, monuments, and things to see there. The first thing needed was to park my RV somewhere close to the Capitol and the Smithsonians. How about the Pentagon? I'm still amazed that no Pentagon security personnel ever bothered me about parking overnight in their huge parking area. I stayed there for three weeks; this was before terrorism. I even took a guided tour through the Pentagon at no cost.

Each morning I would take my bicycle off the back of my motorhome and bike to the Capitol or Smithsonian Museums. I toured the White House and saw the inside of Congress in session. I saw monuments like the Lincoln, Jefferson, and Washington plus the Tomb of the Unknown Soldier. I saw the United States Mint, the Ford Theater, and numerous Smithsonian Museums including Air and Space, Natural History, and American History. Walking through those museums at full speed took me two to three hours each. They were massive and amazing.

I did this for three weeks and saw only a fraction of what was there. My favorite museum was one of the art museums that held precious paintings from centuries past. In 1980 those paintings by the great masters were each valued in the millions of dollars. Today they would each be valued in the tens or hundreds of millions of dollars.

It was a good sightseeing trip with lots of different things to see in one small area. And the timing was good. Getting into the Pentagon now would no doubt require proper ID.

Slick Rock

Slick Rock is a recreation area at Lake Kaweah in California where the river flows into the lake. There's a ban on alcohol at Slick Rock because it's an active and sometimes dangerous area. Each spring the melting snow from surrounding mountains pours cold, swift water into the lake. Alcohol mixed with water recreation can lead to problems.

When I started working at Kaweah as a ranger, I did lots of foot patrol with a warning pad and citation pad. I began using a strategy when I walked Slick Rock. I wanted to stop the beer drinking there without writing lots of tickets. So I began offering the violators a choice. They could allow me to confiscate their beer and receive a warning, or they could keep their beer, put it in their vehicle, and receive a $50 ticket from the Federal government. Very few wanted the ticket.

What I was doing wasn't legal, but the park manager and senior ranger both looked the other way. The beer that I confiscated went into the refrigerator in the staff lunch room. From there the maintenance crew carried it home and drank it. Free beer, what a deal. In this way I minimized my citation paperwork while putting a dent in the beer consumption at Slick Rock.

One day in early summer I was on foot patrol at Slick Rock. The water level was down so the swimming was good and safe. As I walked past a bunch of swimmers, a lady saw my uniform and yelled to me. She waved a wallet at me and said her young son had found it in the river. I took the wet wallet from her, held it in the air, and asked the people in the area if anyone was missing a wallet. Two Hispanic guys on the opposite shore reached into their pockets and one raised his hand. He had lost it. He crossed the river and I asked him to sit. Everybody in the area was now watching with interest.

I gave the fellow a pen and paper and told him to write his name. Then I opened the wallet to check the driver's license. It was a California identification card with a picture on it. I looked at the picture and it looked like him. What I saw next was amazing. The wallet was full of money, at least a quarter-inch thick of wet green bills. He handed me the pen and paper with his scribbled signature. The name matched the ID card.

Before returning the wallet, I beckoned for the young lad who had found it to come and join us. He ran over and I told the Hispanic guy to give the boy five dollars. I put my hand up showing five fingers and told him "cinco." He understood. Everybody is still watching with interest. I returned the wallet and the Hispanic man reached into his wad of bills, pulling out a wet $5 dollar bill. The little boy jumped for joy when he got it and ran to show his mom. I stood up and walked away knowing everybody was happy. The Hispanic guy was very happy about getting his wallet and cash back. The boy was tickled to receive the $5 dollar reward. The spectators were all happy because the boy and the Hispanic man were happy. I was happy because everybody else was happy. This story had a happy ending.

Now for an addendum to this story. I worked as a park ranger for the Corps of Engineers in California for twenty years. During that time I came across lots of lost-and-found items. Numerous lost wallets got returned to their owners, but only twice did I ever see a wallet returned to an owner with any money in it. One recovered wallet had two dollars in it. The other wallet I spoke of here. The odds of that Hispanic fellow's wallet being found in the river were slim. And the odds of that wallet being returned to its owner with any money left in it were even slimmer. That guy had a very lucky day. He was probably a farm worker who had just been paid.

Volunteer Jack

Jack began visiting Eastman Lake when he was in his early 60s. I was working at Eastman then so I met and got to know Jack. He would search for dry driftwood along the shoreline and do wood carving there at the lake. He was a craftsman.

I suggested that he become a volunteer at the lake and live there for free. He could hunt for driftwood and do wood carving whenever he wanted. He thought that sounded like a good idea, he was divorced, so he moved his trailer there. He became the overseer and helper on the lakeside opposite of park headquarters. We outfitted him with a radio and some cleaning equipment and he lived there for the next decade.

Jack kept busy with cleanup and craft work. He would sell his crafts at flea markets. He didn't show any health problems until his mid 70s; then he had a mild stroke. Months later he had trouble walking. The doctors diagnosed him with advanced melanoma skin cancer. Surgery removed a malignant lump on the top of his head, and Jack felt better for a while. Then he lost mobility in his legs again. His son placed him in a veteran's hospital with assisted care in Fresno.

I visited Jack every few weeks in the hospital. We were good friends. The last time I saw him he looked good. His mind was sharp and he was smiling and talking, looking the best I'd seen in months. He told me that his dreams of late had gotten more vivid and real. Sometimes when he woke in the morning, he wasn't sure if he was still dreaming. He said he woke that morning and asked the nurse if she was real or part of a dream he was having.

Two days later I was back at work and told the Eastman staff that Jack looked so good he might make another year. Later that day we got a phone call that he had passed away.

I was surprised because of how good he looked when I saw him. After thinking about his recent vivid dreams, though, I could picture him being in some active dream state and either deciding or being given the choice to stay on the other side. All he had happening in the hospital was lying in bed, unable to walk. Why not choose something else? It was a good time to move on.

Lie Detector Test

The main highway to Sequoia National Park in California runs past Lake Kaweah. Just below Lake Kaweah is a highway intersection with a traffic light and a gas station. That gas station doesn't close because it is so busy with traffic. I knew the owner because I worked at Kaweah. He made big money from that station.

He decided to get a liquor license and sell beer and liquor at his gas station. The female employees working there at night quit because of the increased risk of being robbed. A young man was hired for the night shift. Not long after that, the station was robbed by several men. The investigating police questioned the new employee about the robbers: what they looked like, what clothes they were wearing, how many of them, did he recognize any of them, etc. His answers to the police were so vague that they asked him to come to the police station at a certain date and time to take a lie detector test.

When he didn't show, they checked on him. He disappeared along with the robbers. The police put out a warrant for him and had an idea who the other perpetrators might be. I don't know if any of them were caught.

Summer Baseball – Part 1

After my first year of college, I went to Lincoln, Nebraska, with my best friend, Joe, for the summer. We stayed at his uncle's home. His uncle had two sons, one about ten years old and the other about twelve years old. They liked baseball so the uncle became head coach for a neighborhood baseball team. Joe and I were his assistants.

There was a city baseball league, and the team we fielded entered the league competition. Games were scheduled against other neighborhood teams. It was Little League with age rules and umpires and a game schedule for all the teams.

Our team only had maybe eleven players total or some number like that. We barely had enough neighborhood boys to field a full team. The uncle, Joe, and I gathered them together to figure out what baseball talent they had and what position to play the boys.

The first game we played was all guesswork. We started out with one pitcher. Our team was able to win its first several games and we learned a lot about who could do what. Three of our players could pitch fairly fast if needed. Then we played a game against another undefeated team that was very good. They beat us decisively and showed that they were the better team.

Our games after that – we won them all. Our players were getting better and they began to believe in themselves and believe in the team. They were hitting better, and three of our pitchers could be rotated when needed. At the end of the summer league season, one team was undefeated and our team was in second place with one loss. Our only loss was to the undefeated team.

Rules were that the top two Little League teams would play a final game for the championship. We showed up on game day, and the other team arrived with a big crowd of fans. Everybody expected the undefeated team to win easily. They were all looking confident: the coaches, players, parents, and their fans.

The game started and both teams played well from the start. I don't believe either team committed an error that day. The pitchers for both teams looked sharp. After several innings our team managed to get one or two runs across the plate. It was about the fifth inning when the other team loaded the bases with just one out. Their best hitter came to the plate and hit a scorching one-hop line drive to second base. Our second baseman managed to raise his glove just in time for the ball to slam into it. He then flipped the ball to the shortstop crossing second base who threw to first base for the double play. Everybody was stunned, especially the fans of the other team. They went silent.

The game lasted seven innings and the other team didn't threaten to score again. Our pitchers mowed them down. Our hitters added another one or two runs and we won the game. I think the final score was 3 to 0. We were the city champions and our boys received a team trophy after the game.

The fans, coaches, and players from the other team packed up and left the ball park as quiet as mice. Our players felt like real baseball heroes. The parents of our players couldn't believe how well they had played. Uncle was proud. Joe and I were proud and impressed with how well the team had played. The players and parents were on cloud nine. It was a proud day for all of us.

Summer Baseball – Part 2

There were some interesting stories tied to the Little League baseball team that my friend Joe and I helped coach that summer in Lincoln, Nebraska. We searched the neighborhood for players and found only a dozen prospects at most. Gathering them together, we sorted them out for different playing positions but nobody wanted to play catcher. Finally we picked one boy to be the catcher. He wasn't a good player and he couldn't hit the ball very well but he would have to do. As the season progressed, he improved behind the plate and his confidence grew. By the end of the season he was getting a few hits. In the championship game, which his mother attended, he took a foul tip off his hand. He was crying as we checked it for broken bones. The bones were okay. His mom came over and looked at it and asked us to take him out of the game. We didn't have anybody else to take his place so we told her he would be fine, and we told him to get back in there and catch the ball. The pain would go away. He did.

Joe's uncle had a son about twelve years old who pitched and played shortstop. He pitched the first game and did fine. We won. The second or third game he lost the strike zone so we pitched our third baseman who could throw hard. He did fine. The next game both pitchers had trouble throwing strikes so we tried our first baseman at pitcher. This is what we did for the rest of the season. When a pitcher lost the strike zone, we would rotate the three boys until one of them could throw strikes. None of the three could throw anything except a fast ball. But when they had control, they had speed and were hard to hit.

The second baseman on our team was the youngest son of Joe's uncle, about ten years old. He did okay at fielding and hitting. He was the second baseman who won the championship game for us. He fielded that hot ground ball in the fifth inning with the bases loaded which ended that inning. The other team didn't score. I still remember his big eyes looking like white ping pong balls when that line drive came rocketing toward him.

The most interesting player on the team was our leadoff batter. He was young and very short. He couldn't run fast or throw the ball very well or play infield, so we put him in left field. He never caught a fly ball, but if a batter hit the ball to left field, he would run, get it, and throw it toward the infield. The coaches and players just hoped that no baseballs would be hit to left field.

We batted him leadoff because he was so short. He could barely swing a bat so he never got a hit. In fact, I don't think he ever hit a pitch with his bat, not even a foul ball. But he could get on base. None of the Lincoln Little League pitchers could throw him three strikes in seven pitches, so he walked every time. If his granddad came to a game, he would yell "Swing Johnny" and then the boy would swing and strike out. But his grandpa only went to a few games. We coached the boy to keep the bat on his shoulder and take the walk. When the kid got a walk, our next several batters could hit. That little boy probably had the best on-base batting percentage of any player in the Lincoln Little League that summer. He also probably scored more runs than any other Lincoln Little Leaguer that summer. He didn't realize it but he was one of our most valuable players.

Riverboats

During my traveling years, I sometimes worked on riverboats. Money was/is a necessity. I rode boats mainly on the Illinois and Mississippi rivers, and also the St. Paul waterway. Riverboats push barges filled with bulk commodities like coal, grain, and fuel.

Living and working on a riverboat is not easy. Standard work schedule is thirty days on the boat, thirty days off the boat. Each work day is 6 hours on, 6 hours off, 6 hours on, 6 hours off, every day of the week. Sleeping is difficult. A cook prepares three meals each day. I sometimes worked as a deckhand on tow and sometimes in the engine room as a helper.

I still remember some boat stories. During one trip on the St. Paul canal, a story began to circulate about a missing barge filled with wheat. Value of the wheat was half a million dollars. To pull off a theft like that would require organization, cooperation, planning, and know how. Only an inside group or mob ring or highly skilled bandits with connections could have unloaded a barge full of wheat into a silo and then made that barge disappear.

One night on the Illinois river I was doing deckhand labor when the pilot accidentally rammed the boat into a coal barge. The collision left some large gashes in the outside steel wall of the barge above the water line. I told the pilot about the damage. He shined a light on it and said it was old damage; "Let's go." So we left. That barge needed some serious repair welding. The pilot didn't want the accident on his record. Too much cost and paperwork involved.

Another accident happened going through a lock and dam. A new pilot pushed some empty barges into a lock too fast and hit the upper hand railing on top of the lock gates. The sound was awful. The lock gates weren't damaged but replacing the gate railing probably cost $10,000. A bad start for a new pilot.

I was assisting in the engine room one trip and it was night shift. I filled the incinerator in the engine room with burnable refuse. I also put in a couple of large used fuel filters that were to be thrown away. What I didn't know was that the used fuel filters are not to be burned in a boat incinerator. They burn too hot. I lit the garbage and it quickly got hot. The pilot called down and told me that flames were shooting two feet above the incinerator smoke stack on the roof top. I told him there was nothing I could do but keep watch on it and let the fire burn down.

The two main hazards for all boats, large and small, are sinking and fire. I learned why old filters are not to be burned on boats. This could have developed into a serious engine room fire.

Another time when I was working as an engine room helper, I got diesel fuel in my left eye. I was wearing soft contact lenses and the left lens absorbed some diesel fuel. When I wore that lens, my left eye would get red and inflamed. I finally had to leave that lens out for the remainder of the boat trip. The Chief Engineer looked at my eyes and accused me of smoking marijuana. Smoking marijuana can cause the eyes to redden. I told him to look closely at my eyes. See the red one and see the white one? He did. How can a marijuana smoker get one red eye and one white eye? This puzzled him. Then I told him what happened.

One other story came from a Mississippi river lock and dam. A boss at one of the locks drowned while rowing a boat. He was releasing water from the lock which causes a swirling hole in one area of the river. He then got into a small rowboat and paddled into that strong swirling current and drowned. The only explanation was that the guy committed suicide, but for his family to collect the life insurance money, it had to be an accident.

Vagrancy

I was college age when a friend and I took a trip out of state. We got halfway to our destination, it was late in the evening, so we stopped at a strip mall to get something to eat. Adjacent to the mall was a business building with a number of company trucks in a rear parking lot. We needed gas in our car so we kicked around the idea of stealing gas from one of those trucks. We decided to go have a look.

We crept around the company building to where the trucks were. We were looking to see which trucks had locking gas caps, were they diesel, etc. After just a few minutes of poking around we were suddenly interrupted by flashing lights. Cops were behind us and coming around the other side. A neighbor lady had seen us and called the police.

A policeman asked what we were doing so I told him a lie. I said we were thinking about stealing gas for our car because we had no money and were trying to get back home to Iowa.

The cops cuffed us. I don't recall who drove our car to the police impound lot. We were taken to the police station and placed in a holding cell with several other inmates. It would be a long night ahead. The only cellmate I can still picture was a drunk who was shoved into the holding cell after midnight. He was mad and started shaking the bars, yelling that he was going to burn them out. He would burn them out. This went on for thirty minutes. I'm trying to sleep on a hard bench and so is my friend and this guy is going to burn them out. I had a major headache.

Morning finally came and somebody brought us breakfast. It looked nasty. I wasn't going to eat it but one of the veteran cellmates said they would recycle it and serve it again later if we didn't chop it up. So I took a piece of bread, nibbled on it, and then used it to mix the eggs with the other stuff on the plate.

A policeman cruised by so I got his attention and asked how my friend and I could get out of there. Could we pay a fine and eave? He said he would check. A while later he came back and told us we weren't charged with burglary; we were locked up for vagrancy. I asked him what the fine was and he said $35. I told him we would both pay the fine; we wanted out. This surprised him because he assumed we had no money. He said he would get the paperwork ready.

A short time later he came back and let us out of jail. We were taken to a desk and presented with citations for vagrancy. We both paid the money, got a receipt, picked up our car keys, and left. Then we gassed up our car and headed out of town toward our destination.

It was weeks before I got back to Iowa. When I did return home, I talked with mom and dad about different things. I told mom about getting thrown into jail for vagrancy. Mom shared that story with one of her card-playing friends who was a lawyer and he told mom that the police couldn't charge me for vagrancy if I had money. The police had wronged me. Mom told me that the next day; the cops had violated my rights.

She mentioned it again several more times over the next couple of days; the cops had no lawful right to charge me with vagrancy if I had money. Finally I told her how it really went down. My friend and I were checking out some trucks to try and steal some gas. The cops caught us. I lied to the cops and told them we needed to get back home but had no money. They threw us in jail and charged us not for burglary but for vagrancy. We paid the tickets and left there pronto.

After that I didn't hear any more from mom about the police violating my rights.

Seeing Auras

Everybody has an aura and everybody can see auras. It is simple and easy to do for anyone, young and old. I'm going to explain how you can do it in five minutes time.

Find a person who wants you to see their aura. Get a chair and place it in front of a light-colored background. The background should be light-colored but not bright white. Don't have a cluttered background with windows, pictures, or other distractions. Your starting point is to have a subject sitting in a chair in front of a clean light-colored background.

Now sit in a chair facing your subject at a distance of about 10-15 feet. Look two inches above the top of your subject's head, and then spread your eyes apart just a little. You're not focusing your vision on anything. You're just looking obliquely with eyes spread apart. This is the same way you look at a three-dimensional flat picture. When looking at a 3D picture, you spread your eyes apart just a little and wait. You're doing the same thing here. Look two inches above the person's head in the same way you would look at a 3D picture. Hold that oblique gaze and remain still. This is not difficult to do. Whenever you blink and lose that oblique vision, just reestablish it and continue and wait. Don't do anything else. It's easy.

Within minutes you will begin to see a very thin bright white light around your subject's head. This thin light will be very bright and easy to see. Keep your vision oblique. Outward from the thin bright light will be a softer light extending a couple of inches above the person's head. The aura you're seeing will probably be white but it may show some color as well.

So there – you've done it, and it took you five minutes. If you become interested in auras, there's more you can read about colored auras. The color of a person's aura may indicate something about that person's health or personality. I've seen auras colored white, yellow, blue, and green.

When I visited my brother in Utah a few years ago, we drove to see his oldest daughter to say hi. Her husband showed up. We were sitting in the living room and I suggested we check out the daughter's aura. She sat down on the floor in front of a light-colored wall and I told everyone to look two inches above her head, then spread the eyes apart just a little. Her husband could see her aura very easily which impressed him. When I looked at her aura, it was so strong that I didn't need to look at it obliquely. I could look straight at her face, without spreading my eyes, and see a white light around her head.

Before I retired from the Corps of Engineers in California, I sometimes took airplane flights to training conferences. Sitting for hours on a plane can be boring so I sometimes looked at the auras of passengers sitting in front of me. On one flight I could see a strong white light around the head of an elderly gentleman several seats in front of me. When I got off the plane, he walked past me in the hallway so I told him that while sitting behind him I could see a strong white aura around his head. He thanked me very much for saying that; it made him feel good.

On another flight I was seated across from the wife of another park ranger who was on the plane. She asked me to check out her aura and see what color it was. A young lady sitting between us said she wanted to learn that so I told her to look two inches above the lady's head and then spread her eyes apart. Hold that. I did the same and told the wife that I could see her aura and it had a yellowish tint to it. The young lady in the middle sounded off with glee. She was also seeing an aura with a yellowish color. All of a sudden she could see auras.

Bulldog Blitz

I buy season tickets to the Fresno State University football games each year. I've followed all of the Fresno State Bulldog sports teams for the past decade. About five years ago Fresno State added a new twist to their home football games. Just prior to game time, a sky-diving team would jump into the stadium. The announcer would say "And now it's time for the Bulldog Blitz. Look up in the sky." On a large stadium screen fans could see live coverage of the girls jumping and free falling. Then we all look up in the sky and here they come, parachutes open, one after the other.

My stadium seat is top row in the end zone so I can see everything. The parachutes fly in over my head and the announcer calls out their names. Sarah from Madera sails in, then Brandi, then the others.

A couple of years ago Sarah from Madera and her father were parachuting into an olive festival at Madera, a city nearby. Her father jumped out of the airplane first and Sarah followed. The father's first chute failed so he cut away and pulled his reserve cord. His reserve chute got fouled and he hit the ground head first. Sarah was coming down in her chute above him so she saw everything happen in real time.

Sarah didn't quit parachuting, though. That year there were three Bulldog parachuters, all females. Today we only have two jumpers, Sarah from Madera and Brandi.

One of the 2021 football games I went early, and in a reserve parking lot I saw three young adults putting on red/white/blue jump suits. They had to be the Bulldog Blitz. I went over and asked which one was Sarah from Madera. She looked up and said hi; a nice-looking gal. Brandi was there also, another beauty, plus a third young man in a jump suit. They were going to jump at halftime rather than the start of the game. Putting on a tattered pair of coveralls was another attractive young lady who said she was flying the airplane. I knew she was a parachute jumper as well. An older man with them was the navigator.

I told all of them that the Bulldog fans love them. It is a thrill watching them fly into the stadium. Sometimes one of them will sail over my head and fly through the goal posts. Most of their landings are standup in the center of the field. They always get a huge round of applause.

My brother, Dale, will love this story. He was a jumper in his younger years.

You're Fired

I took off for Los Angeles with a friend one summer between college years. We drove his car and pulled a trailer behind it carrying his motorcycle and my motorcycle. Finding an apartment in LA wasn't easy because he had a dog, we both had motorcycles, and we were college age. When we finally got settled, we began looking around for summer jobs. At a strip mall not far from where we lived, the workers at a grocery store were on strike, picketing outside. For us it looked like a job opportunity and we needed money, so we went inside and applied. They hired both of us on the spot.

My friend was tasked with working in the produce area, taking care of fruits and vegetables. I helped with sacking groceries for customers and stocking shelves with food items. Things went well the first day although the picketers outside didn't like us. We arrived for work the second day and went about our business. In the afternoon my friend came over to me with a big smile on his face. He told me he had a cold beer hidden on the side and was sipping it while working with his fruits and vegetables. I thought that was a good idea so I went and got a cold bottle of beer and took it in the restroom and drank some. Suddenly a boss man came into the restroom so I quickly hid the beer behind a toilet. He looked at me and asked what I was doing there. I left and went back to stocking shelves. A few minutes later the boss man walked up to me and said "Drinking on the job. You're fired." He had found my open bottle of beer behind the toilet. Then he went over to my friend and told him the same thing "Drinking on the job. You're fired." So we were both fired.

We took off our work aprons and went over to the bookkeeper and she paid us for two days work. The money helped but now we needed jobs again. There was a road construction project happening about thirty miles away that we'd seen so we drove there the following day. It was early afternoon when we got there and a very hot day, at least 100 degrees. We parked his car at the job site, wondering if we wanted to work there in that heat. Just then a beetle flew down and bounced on the hood of the car and got flipped on its back. This bug was huge, an inch long and fat. We watched as the beetle wiggled its legs trying to upright itself. In less than a minute that bug fried to death from the heat. We looked at each other wondering if this was a message.

We decided to ask about work anyway. One fellow we talked to knew the young boss in charge and he introduced us. The young boss said he could use two laborers to carry some heavy metal rebars. He hired us and we put on gloves and went to work. There were some heavy rebars being bent by a machine and we had to manually pick them up, one at a time, and carry them from point A to point B. The heat was stifling and both of us were tired after just a couple of hours. When the work shift ended, we bought a cold six-pack of beer on the way home that tasted so refreshing.

The next day my friend and I showed up for a full day of work and we did the same thing. The heat was 100 degrees and we were beat after eight hours. I was feeling heat exhaustion. We talked it over and decided this work was too hard and too hot for us. We wouldn't survive here for very long. So we went to the young boss man and told him we were quitting; we found better jobs closer to home. He was disappointed but paid us for two days work.

Now we needed jobs again. I searched around and finally interviewed for work with the city of Los Angeles. I managed to get a job washing police cars for the LAPD. That work I could handle. I stayed with that job for the remainder of the summer. Then it was time to head back to Iowa State University for another year of college.

Kit Carson

I watched a television series awhile back about young kids and reincarnation. A boy two years old was having recurring nightmares and couldn't sleep. When he first began to talk, he would tell his mother about the same nightmare he was having each night. He would see a man being killed, then the wife and daughter of the man were both killed, and then their bodies were burned. He was the one who killed them and burned their bodies. He didn't like going to sleep because he would see this same scene over and over.

The mother began to wonder if there could be a reincarnation connection to the frightening dreams. She asked the boy questions as he grew. By the time the boy was 5 or 6 years old she had learned more about the bad dreams. The boy said he was a young soldier in the dream, and he had mistakenly killed an important man who looked like an Indian. The young soldier was told by an officer to kill the man's wife and daughter so nobody would know. He did this and then burned the bodies to get rid of any evidence. Afterwards the young soldier was tormented by guilt for the rest of his life.

The boy finally came up with a name. He said the young soldier's name was Kit. The mother searched on the computer and found an explorer/soldier named Kit Carson. She showed the picture of Kit Carson to the boy and he said "yes", that was him.

No historian or writer of Kit Carson lore has ever written anything about this story mentioned above. If true, this would be a new Kit Carson story, something not known before. Kit Carson has always been described as a respected frontiersman, explorer, and soldier who was involved in Indian affairs and Indian wars during the middle 1800s. All the native tribes of the southwest U.S. knew of Carson, in particular the Navajo and Utes.

Another interesting story about Kit Carson comes from the PBS television series "Antiques Roadshow". I saw an episode where a fellow brought in an Indian blanket for appraisal. The Roadshow expert looked at the blanket and was very impressed. He declared t a genuine Navajo blanket woven for an important Ute chief. It was old, dating back to the mid 1800s, and in very good condition.

The man who owned the blanket said it had passed down through families from Kit Carson himself. Evidently the Navajo Indians had presented the blanket to Carson because they considered him of chief status. The Utes called him Little Chief. The man said he had no documentation of ownership by Kit Carson, however.

The Roadshow appraiser told the man that even without documentation showing ties to Kit Carson, the blanket was so rare and in such good condition that it could bring $350,000-500,000 at auction. The man who owned it was flabbergasted; he couldn't believe it. He said he and the previous owners never had money.

That Navajo/Ute Indian blanket was indeed put up for auction and was shown on the "Antiques Roadshow" in a museum for public display. It sold for $490,000 without documented ties to Kit Carson.

Water Safety

My first job assignment when I started working as a park ranger at Lake Kaweah in CA was teaching water safety in schools. Every Corps of Engineers lake has an interpretive park ranger who does this. I put together a water safety program and began scheduling presentations for elementary schools in the area.

My second or third year of doing this, I hooked up with a young lady who was in a wheelchair. She had broken her neck diving into shallow water and could no longer walk. She wanted to tell the kids about being safe and smart around water. We were a good team for several years and most of the newspapers covered our water safety visits to the schools. In one case we made the local television news.

1996 was a summer Olympics year, and that spring I was scheduled to fly to Florida for a national water safety conference. It was a glorified week vacation, courtesy of the U.S. Army Corps of Engineers. Three things happened during that trip that are worth retelling.

First, on one of my Florida airplane flights, there were some young ladies on the plane wearing U.S. Olympic jackets. I asked if they were on the U.S. Olympic team and they said yes, the softball team. I had never heard of the U.S.A. winning a softball medal so I assumed that our team wasn't very strong. I told them good luck, the fans in America would be cheering them on, and have fun. When the Olympics got underway that summer, I learned that softball had just been added as a new Olympic sport. Our girls won the gold medal.

A second memory from that water safety conference came when a speaker asked for ideas about how to reduce water accidents at Corps lakes. I raised my hand, stood up, and told the audience that taking the sale of alcohol out of their marina leases would help. Some Corps lakes have marinas, and those marinas are contracted by the U.S. Army Corps of Engineers. After the conference, the Seattle District did just that; they took the sale of alcohol out of their marina leases. It was a first for the Corps of Engineers in America.

A third memory from that conference I won't forget and it still holds true today. The manager of Lake Mead gave a presentation and talked about water accidents at his lake. Lake Mead is a massive lake behind Boulder Dam which isn't far from Las Vegas and Henderson, Nevada. He mentioned that floating bodies are routinely found in different parts of Lake Mead which are attributed to mob killings. When quizzed about the number of floaters found annually at Lake Mead, he gave a number of approximately thirty.

Everybody has heard of ties between Las Vegas money and organized crime. Apparently Lake Mead has become a prime dumping zone for mob killings. The current average is about two bodies per month, and that number may be low.

Citizen Arrest

I drove from Lake Kaweah to the nearby town of Three Rivers one day to gas up a ranger pickup. The road from Kaweah through Three Rivers goes to Sequoia National Park so it is a busy, winding, two lane highway. On my way back to the lake, I caught up to a car traveling very slow. Speed limit is 55 mph and this car was driving 30 mph with no passing lane. I followed for several miles wondering why the driver was going so slow. Finally the car pulled over in a pullout area so I did, too. I would check and see if the driver was okay.

I was dressed in my park ranger uniform and walked to the car where an adult lady had her window rolled down. When she started talking, I knew immediately what the problem was. I told her to wait there, then went back to my truck and called for a sheriff deputy. She got out of her car so I went back over to her and suggested we both walk a straight line. Could she walk a straight line behind me? She tried but didn't do very well.

The sheriff deputy on patrol at Lake Kaweah showed up. He asked her a couple of questions and then called for the California Highway Patrol to come and deal with this DUI case. I left the scene and returned to Kaweah park headquarters.

About twenty minutes later I got a radio call from the deputy; where was I? A CHP officer and the sheriff deputy met me at park headquarters. The problem they had was that neither of them had seen the lady driving.

I told them I was driving back from Three Rivers and had stopped behind her to check on her welfare. She was driving 30 mph on a busy highway.

The CHP officer said he tested her and she was intoxicated. He told me he was going to write it up as a citizen arrest. I had seen her driving but Corps park rangers don't carry guns or make arrests, so I was making a citizen arrest. Later the sheriff deputy told me the lady had gotten belligerent with both officers, telling them "Yes, I'm drunk. What of it?" She also said she was currently enrolled in an alcohol treatment program. That apparently wasn't helping her.

Parachutes and Hang Gliders

When I first started traveling around the U.S. in a motorhome during the 1970s, I visited my brother, Dale, living in San Bernardino, CA. He was doing some skydiving at Elsinore then, not far away, so I decided to give it a try.

I drove to the Elsinore airfield and paid for beginner skydiving lessons. Cost was less than $100 which included five jumps. There were perhaps eight people in my beginner group, and we began with several hours of ground training. When landing in a parachute, you keep your vision forward, not looking at the ground below, and you have your knees touching together to get a better and safer tumble and roll. When the training ended, we all suited up and boarded an airplane.

One of the instructors went with us as a spotter and person in charge. We were all nervous but also confident that we weren't going to die. In just a few minutes the plane reached 3500 feet and the first beginner was attached to a static line. I didn't volunteer to go first. All beginners are attached by static line to the airplane so their rip cords are pulled automatically. Only experienced skydivers are allowed to jump and free fall.

The first jumper hung out the open door in proper flying position and then let go. The spotter watched the action unfold. When that jumper landed safely, the next beginner did the same thing. We all took a turn at getting attached to the static line and then hanging outside the airplane door. Nobody chickened out. When I let go, I tried to keep my head back and my arms and legs spread for stability in the air. I got a good look at the spotter and waved at him just before my rip cord was pulled. When my parachute opened, it gave me a jolt. Then it was a downward float to the ground, lasting maybe a minute. The view was a thrill. As I approached the ground, I kept my eyes forward and held my knees together. My feet hit the ground and I did a gentle roll and tumble. No damage.

I made four jumps that day. My second, third, and fourth were not so good. I twisted and rolled after leaving the plane and didn't have much flight stability. The spotter liked my first jump but not my last three.

The following year I was on the other side of the country, driving along the coast of North Carolina. In the city of Kitty Hawk I saw a big sign offering hang-gliding lessons, five flights for about $40. I thought, why not, so I stopped and paid the fee. The sand dunes and coastal winds in that area make hang-gliding a popular sport there. I was in a group of 5-10 beginners, with one instructor and one hang glider.

The hang-gliding lessons and flights turned out to be more work than anything else. Our hang glider was heavy and we would run with it into the wind, hoping to lift off a sandy incline. Sometimes one of us would get level and airborne for a short distance. But the majority of our attempts were nose dives, right or left, into the sand. A nose dive was considered a flight. I don't recall if I got a clean short flight or not; maybe one. It was more of a workout for everybody, but at least we tried. We could always say that we had done it; we had hang-glided.

Mom Gone

I drove to Slick Rock recreation area at Lake Kaweah one afternoon to do some foot patrol. I parked my ranger truck at the first parking lot and opened my car door. Just then I heard someone by the river shout "She's drowning." I grabbed the car radio and alerted the Kaweah office to a possible drowning at Slick Rock. I would get back to them as soon as possible when I learned more. I ran to the river about forty yards away where there were numerous people. They told me a young woman had slipped off a rock into the cold river current minutes earlier. She hadn't been seen since.

From my hand radio I called the Kaweah office: notify Kaweah boat patrol of a drowning in progress at Slick Rock and also call the local sheriff deputy in nearby Three Rivers city. Then I and some others started scouting the river's edge for a swimmer or a body.

The Three Rivers deputy arrived in ten minutes and brought a medical lady with him. A short time later the Kaweah boat patrol showed up in their boat. They had trouble navigating the river current while using a pike pole to fish for a body. The medical lady took three little girls away from the river's edge and up to the parking area. They were children of the missing mother, ages maybe three to six years old. I left the shoreline and went to the parking area where the children were. The boyfriend of the missing mother showed up and he saw my ranger uniform. He asked me what was happening. I explained the situation to him and got information from him about who the missing mother was. By this time, thirty minutes had elapsed and no body had been found. I still remember looking at the three little girls beside the medical lady. They didn't understand the gravity of what had happened to their mom. The oldest one was saying "Did they find her yet?"

The boyfriend headed down to the river, and a short while later I left the scene. The missing mother was not found that afternoon. An hour later everybody called it quits and went home. I wrote up an incident report for the Kaweah Corps of Engineers.

It was two weeks later when the young woman's body was recovered. She was floating at the river's edge not far from where she had fallen in. The county coroner came and retrieved the body. The following day Kaweah headquarters received a FAX of the coroner's report. The mother had been smoking marijuana.

Days after the incident I saw the Three Rivers deputy and asked him about the three young daughters. He told me a relative had taken all three girls; they were still together. He said the new mother was a good lady and she had a good home.

The Widowmaker

Motorcycle hill climbs are fun to watch. A biker starts at the bottom of a hill and tries to ride his motorcycle as high up the hill as he can. It's a simple strategy. The motorcycle that goes the highest wins. If more than one rider climbs to the top, the quickest time wins.

I entered a couple of hill climbs when I was in college. Some friends and I did the best we could on a very challenging hill. It took two years before someone went over the top of that hill on a motorcycle.

1964 was when the Widowmaker Hill Climb got started at Draper, Utah. It was a formidable hill; very few riders made it to the top. It drew more and more riders and spectators with each passing year. By the 1970s every motorcycle hill climber in America had heard of the Widowmaker.

I happened to be traveling through Utah one year in the 1970s when I learned that the Widowmaker Hill Climb was happening at Draper. I drove there and located the event, paid my entrance fee, and parked my RV amongst hundreds of other vehicles. There were thousands of people there and bikers everywhere.

Looking at the hill was a bit scary. It was covered with scrub vegetation and gullies. The first 1100 feet was inclined with lots of vegetation mounds. Beyond that was a short but steeper incline called the "wall". Only an upright motorcycle with speed could climb the "wall". Past the "wall" was an incline that was doable if the bike and rider had forward momentum. Top of the hill was 1500 feet.

The Widowmaker event that I saw took most of the day to complete. Each rider got only one attempt at the hill; that's how many motorcycles there were. The riders were rough and tough, skilled bike handlers. The motorcycles they brought were even more impressive. Half the bikes had elongated frames with rear wheel scoops and plenty of power. Some had no rubber tires on the rear wheel. When those guys revved up at the starting gate and took off at high throttle, the rear wheel scoops threw dirt twenty feet in the air. It was something to witness.

All the way up the hill were helpers wearing yellow shirts. They assisted getting the bikes back down the hill. At the starting block was an announcer on a loud speaker who called the action and the rider's names. At the top of the hill was a timing light for those who made it that far. Thousands of spectators were scattered everywhere, even halfway up the left side of the hill. Beer was flowing.

The first riders had an obvious disadvantage of plowing through vegetation. After about twenty riders, the path up the hill became more visible and doable. Some of the crashes were spectacular, with bikes and riders flying through the air.

Several bikers made it over the top at the event I saw. Bikes with smaller engines made it to 900 feet. The big bikes with extended frames made it to 1100 feet. Only a few bikers got above 1200 feet. Winning prize was several thousand dollars. The top ten places paid good money. First rider to the top received a bonus of $1000.

Reflecting on the event brings back some memories. The beer drinking was excessive and no doubt a highway problem afterward. Midway through the climb a drunk spectator halfway up the hill wandered over to the motorcycle path. The rider at the starting gate saw him and paid no attention. He started up the hill at full throttle, with perfect handling, throwing up dirt on a perfect line past the drunk and on up the hill. He missed the drunk by three feet, after which the drunk guy got down on his knees and started bowing up and down. He was having a time. The announcer on the loud speaker told the yellow-shirt helpers to get that guy off the hill because he might get hit and spoil a good bike run.

The Widowmaker Hill Climb became the premier motorcycle hill-climb attraction in America until 1988. That year there were so many problems involving alcohol that Draper city officials refused to issue permits for the event the next year, and following years. It was a sad ending for the Widowmaker because the bikers loved the event and they loved the hill. It was a challenge.

Footnote: Anyone interested in seeing some of the Widowmaker Hill Climb action can do so on the computer. Do a search on the web or on youtube for Widowmaker Hill Climb.

Black Bulls

Eastman Lake is a Corps of Engineers lake in central California. I worked there for many years before I retired. Part of the flood control responsibility of Eastman Lake is managing several small earthen dams a few miles to the north.

One contract that Eastman Lake oversees for all of its dams is trapping for beavers, muskrats, and other varmints below the dams. A contractor was hired for this and he drove his brand-new SUV vehicle to the small earthen dams north of Eastman Lake. He was given a key and permission to park on adjacent property, which was a green pasture with grazing Angus bulls. He left his vehicle there and walked a distance to check for muskrats and rodents below the dams.

While he was gone, the black bulls became interested in his vehicle. They took turns rubbing their sides and backs on the SUV. And these bulls were full grown, weighing 2000 pounds each. They spent time itching, scratching, and rubbing, and when the contractor came back, his vehicle looked like an accordion. None of the doors would open. The only way he could drive it home was to break out a window and crawl inside.

When he got home, he notified the insurance company and they wanted an explanation for the damage. The only thing he could tell them in his written report was that he had parked in the wrong place. The insurance company totaled out the car.

Hurricane Katrina

John and Doris were campground hosts for two years at Eastman Lake when I worked there. We became friends and kept in touch after they left. They were retired and lived in a fifth-wheel trailer which they parked on the southern coast of Mississippi. They had lived in southern Mississippi for many years and were accustomed to Gulf storms.

Hurricane Katrina happened in late 2005 and it was well advertised. Everybody followed the Katrina forecasts. The only thing not known about Katrina was where it would hit land. Initially Katrina was spinning toward Houston so John and Doris decided to hunker down. Then Katrina changed directions and turned toward New Orleans. John still had time to hook up and move their trailer inland, but they elected to stay.

When Katrina hit land, all the coastline from Texas to Florida suffered from storm surge. Water and waves rose twenty feet where John and Doris were parked. They watched the storm waves rise higher and higher. When the water reached their fifth-wheel trailer, a neighbor on higher ground got a small boat and ferried them to his place. From there they watched the storm surge continue until it eventually lifted and carried their fifth-wheel and pickup out into the Gulf. They lost everything they owned.

I talked to Doris on the phone several weeks later. She and John were living then with relatives in Arkansas. Doris said John was a broken man after Katrina. He couldn't forgive himself for not driving his pickup and trailer to safety. His health was declining and both of them were doing poorly. They were now dependent on relatives and wondering what to do and where to go next.

Timmy

When I worked at Eastman Lake in CA, I sometimes scheduled evening programs for campers on summer weekends. Eastman Lake's campground has a small but nice amphitheater with seating and a stage.

There are horse trails at Eastman and a primitive campground adjacent to the main campground. One day I drove my park ranger truck through the primitive campground and saw a lady setting up camp. She had a nice horse so I stopped and made her an offer. If she would do a campground program that evening with her horse, she could camp for free. I told her she could use her own judgment whether or not to allow kids and others to sit on her horse. She agreed.

That afternoon I advertised the horse program in the campground with flyers and the lady showed up with her horse. All went well and she let the kids get up on her horse. They enjoyed it and she did, too.

A week later I saw a new rider and horse at the lake and following behind the big horse was a miniature donkey. I knew immediately this was something special. I stopped and talked to the lady rider. I told her I wanted her to do a campground program with the little donkey. I would give her free camping and she could bring her big horse. If she wanted to let the kids and adults sit on the big horse, that was her choice. Her decision was a go. It sounded like fun so we set a date and time.

That coming weekend she arrived in the primitive campground and I handed out flyers to the campers. In the afternoon she walked her horse and donkey through the campground for advertisement. When the program started there were lots of kids and adults there. She showed the audience her big horse and talked about safety and being kind to horses and animals. Then she brought the little donkey up on stage. His name was Timmy and she talked about him for a few minutes. Then she invited everyone to come up on stage and get a closer look and touch if they wanted to.

Like an avalanche, the kids swarmed onto the stage to get at Timmy: talking to him, petting and rubbing him, pulling his mane and tale. Timmy was an instant hit. A couple of kids may have gotten on his back. The lady let some of the kids set atop her big horse. It was a great show. The kids and people enjoyed it and so did the lady. I brought her and Timmy back a number of times after that for Eastman campground shows.

Magic Man

One summer at Eastman Lake I recruited a magic man for a summer campground program. I learned about him from another park ranger. He lived a distance away so I called him and offered him free camping for a weekend if he would come to Eastman and do one magic show. He said okay, so we picked a busy holiday weekend for his magic act.

He and his family and relatives showed up and they were given two prime campsites next to the campground amphitheater. I advertised the show that afternoon in the campground which was full. At showtime the amphitheater was packed. The magician brought his wife on stage as an assistant. The rest of his family group sat in the audience.

He began his show by pulling birds out of his hat and pockets. Then he started making things disappear. Kids in the front row were going crazy trying to figure out how things can disappear. He did a variety of magic tricks that were entertaining. He brought a volunteer on stage and had the volunteer hold some large metal rings. The magician took hold of the metal rings with the volunteer and they waved the rings back and forth. The rings would lock together, then unlock, then lock again. The volunteer holding the rings was watching this happen but he couldn't figure out how it was being done. The magician ended his show with a fire trick.

The program lasted about forty-five minutes, and it was so good that people in the audience came up to me afterward and asked if they should have paid. I told them it was free. They were impressed; a free magic show in a park campground.

Vertigo

I was in my late 60s when I began noticing spells of light-headedness. By my early 70s these periods of mild dizziness had become more frequent and irritating. I made the assumption that it must be old age. Maybe I would be plagued by mild vertigo for the remainder of my life.

Then I watched a documentary on Amazon Prime titled "The Brain that Changes Itself". This documentary shows that the brain has more potential for brain repair than most people realize.

The theme of the documentary is brain plasticity, meaning that the brain can change itself. School kids with mental deficiencies were wearing a patch over one eye while doing their homework and testing. Their schooling improved. A lady with severe loss of movement was given a specific eye task on a regular schedule. She gradually regained her normal mobility.

The way this happens is that if one side of the brain begins to malfunction, the other side of the brain can rectify the problem. The good side of the brain can create new paths of signal communication to override or bypass the bad brain signals.

To better understand this, we first need to know that all visual information coming through the right eye travels to the left half of the brain. And vice versa: all visual information coming through the left eye travels to the right half of the brain. Let's pose an example. If there is a brain malfunction happening in the right side of the brain, we can attempt to fix this by covering the left eye. Doing this will funnel all visual information and brain processing through the right eye to the left half of the brain.

With the left eye covered, we now need to make the brain think and work. I can do this by playing scrabble on my computer with one eye patched. Other people may want to do crossword puzzles or play some other game that requires thinking. Doing this with the left eye covered forces all thinking and visual info through the right eye to the left side of the brain. The left brain can then activate tasks that the right brain would normally do. The opposite of this happens if the right eye is covered. Whatever malfunction is happening in the brain, using an eye patch may bring about a fix.

People with vertigo issues or movement problems should try this. Patch one eye for a couple of hours one day and force the brain to think and work. Then patch the other eye the next day for a couple of hours and force the brain to think and work. See if either one helps. Does patching one eye help more than patching the other eye? When I first tried this, I noticed improvement in my vertigo within a couple of days. It may sound too easy to be true, but give it a try. You have nothing to lose and you may see surprising improvement. Positive results can happen quickly.

Still a Mystery

I was working alone at Eastman Lake one afternoon and received a phone call from the police department. They asked me to check on suspicious activity at one of the boat docks. They had received a call from a concerned fisherman. I was to call them back and let them know if they needed to send a policeman.

I drove to the boat dock and nobody was there. Parked on the boat ramp was a pickup truck with a boat trailer backed into the water. There was no boat, no driver, and the truck engine was running. I moved the truck and trailer to the parking lot. Then I drove back to the office and called the police department. I told them to send a cop to Eastman Lake because something looked amiss.

Twenty minutes later a police car showed up. I explained the situation to the cop and gave him the truck keys. He found a cell phone in the passenger seat of the truck and began looking through it. I drove my ranger truck back to the office and hooked up the ranger patrol boat. By the time the policeman and I got the ranger boat in the water, the sun was going down.

I navigated the boat slowly around the upper half of the lake, using a spotlight to avoid hazards. The only boater we found told us he had made the phone call to the police. After a two-hour search in the dark, I took the patrol boat back to the dock and trailered it. I told the patrolman I was headed back to the office to call my bosses and write a report. Then I was off duty. The case was his.

At the office I called the park manager and the district manager and told them about the missing boater. Then I wrote a report and went home.

The following morning the missing boat was located, floating near the dam. But the boater was still missing. The police department brought out a dive team for an underwater search, starting at the boat ramp where the truck and trailer had been parked. In a short time they found the fisherman's body in six feet of water near the boat ramp.

We never did figure out what happened. Did the guy fall and hit his head, or did he hit the boat throttle wrong, or just slip and fall in the water? It was a mystery.

Mexico

Twice I've been across the border into Mexico. I spent a summer in Los Angeles with a college friend and we decided to go to Tijuana. Neither of us had been to Mexico and we knew the risks. We drove to the border and parked our car on the U.S. side. Then we checked through customs and walked across the border. We wanted to buy a couple of fake IDs because we weren't yet twenty-one years old, so we talked to a Mexican cab driver. He said he would take us to a place that could make us some IDs if we paid him a few dollars. We agreed and he drove us to a flop house not far away.

Before entering the dumpy flop house, we hid all our money. I put some of my money in my shoe and the rest in my sock. When we went inside, there was a row of rooms and a nice-looking gal sitting on a bench in the hallway. A Mexican guy about thirty years old came up to us and asked what we wanted. We told him we wanted some fake IDs. He took us into a room and said it could be done and gave us a price. We told him the price was too high so he told us to wait there for a minute. He left the room and then a big Mexican bouncer came in. He told us to give him all of our money. We objected; my friend was almost as big as he was. The bouncer gave my friend a light karate chop across his throat and we didn't argue anymore. I showed the guy that my wallet was empty but he found the money in my shoe. He got most of the money my friend had and then told us to leave. On our way out I remember the lady in the hallway looking at us like we were two fools. And she was right.

Outside we still had a little money so we walked to a bar not far away and bought one beer. Bar girls came over to us and wanted money for some action. A Mexican guy with a flashlight kept making rounds to see if our beer bottles were empty. When we left there, we walked past several more sleazy bars on our way back to our car. Well-dressed Mexican men on the sidewalk asked us what we were looking for: women, booze, drugs, what? We didn't tell them that the flop house down the street had already robbed us of most of our money.

My only other trip into Mexico was after college when I spent a winter working in south Texas. I decided to drive my car across the border to Monterrey for a couple of days. Monterrey wasn't a border town and therefore less risky for tourists. I wanted to get a look inside Mexico.

At the border crossing a Mexican official said I would have to do some paperwork but he couldn't get to it right away. So I went and sat down for ten minutes until he finally decided that I could do the paperwork. What he really wanted was a five-dollar payoff to expedite the paperwork. I gave him nothing and waited for him to do his job.

Then I drove to Monterrey. In the city I saw a young Mexican man standing on a street corner with a big smile on his face so I stopped and asked if he was a tour guide. He said yes. I asked how much and we agreed on $10 per day. He got in my car and showed me some sights and got me to a motel. I offered him another $10 for the next day. After two days of seeing Monterrey, I was ready to leave.

Driving back to the U.S., my car was inspected at the border and then I crossed into Texas. A few miles north of the border a police car fell in behind me and flashed its lights. I pulled over and two cops did a thorough search of my car. They saw my Iowa license plates and suspected a drug connection. All I had was a few cheap tourist souvenirs that I'd purchased in Monterrey. They even lifted the hood of my car and looked around my engine for contraband.

So that was my experience of seeing the interior of Mexico. What I know of Mexico is mostly what I've heard, read, or seen on television. It is a country suffering from poverty. Where there is widespread poverty, there is rampant corruption and crime. Mexico fits that bill. It is not a safe place for outsiders to visit.

Houseboat Hero

When I started working at Lake Kaweah in 1991, one of my park ranger duties was houseboat inspections. I inspected all the houseboats at the marina annually and got to know the owners.

I was only a few months into the job when I heard a story about one of the houseboat owners. A young man told me that days earlier his father had taken his houseboat out on the lake near the dam with some friends. They saw a small boat on the lake begin to take on water with people on board. The father started the houseboat engine and powered toward the sinking vessel. One by one seven people were pulled from the water onto the houseboat. The capsized boat went to the bottom of the lake. None of the seven people had life jackets, and none could swim.

I could hardly believe what I was hearing. Seven people who couldn't swim had rowed a small, overloaded boat out into deep water without lifejackets, and the boat capsized. None drowned because a houseboat got to them first.

I wrote down names and pertinent information from the son and immediately called the newspaper in the nearby city of Three Rivers. The houseboat owner lived there. I told them there was a hero living in their city and they needed to write a story about him.

The newspaper jumped on it. They were at Lake Kaweah within the hour and took my information about the incident. Then they went to the houseboat owner's home and got the full story from him. The next newspaper issue had a big splash with pictures about the local resident who saved the lives of seven people at Lake Kaweah.

I saw the son again a week later and asked about his dad and the news article. The son said his dad soaked it up. Everybody in town congratulated him for saving those people's lives. The cheers he got in Three Rivers had him walking on air for a while.

Flying Tiger

I met an interesting fellow one day at a Lake Kaweah recreation area. A family group had taken him out for a day trip. He looked about seventy-five years old and told me he was a war veteran. I told him my dad flew in World War 2 and that got him started. He, too, had flown in WW2 and he started with the Flying Tigers in China. China needed pilots and airplanes back then, so a U.S. military officer named Claire Chennault helped train Chinese pilots and also helped acquire airplanes and volunteer pilots from America to aid the Chinese war effort. After Japan bombed Pearl Harbor, the Flying Tigers in China were assimilated into the U.S. Navy and Air Force.

I asked him the obvious question: how many Japanese planes did he shoot down? He told me he only shot down one plane as a Flying Tiger. But during the Marianas Turkey Shoot in the Philippines, June of 1944, he shot down five Japanese Zeros. When the war ended, he had eight kills which made him an Ace.

The most interesting part of his story was the Turkey Shoot. I've seen many WW2 documentaries over the years, and this guy told me something I'd never heard before. He said that when the U.S. military targeted the Mariana Islands for air raids, some of the Japanese planes there didn't have bullets. American pilots could see Zeros flying and dodging around but doing no shooting. Afterward the assumption was made that some Japanese planes either had limited ammunition or none at all. There were Japanese planes in the Turkey Shoot that did have ammunition, of course; 30 U.S. warplanes were shot down. But the Japanese lost 350 planes in that battle, and according to this Flying Tiger who was there, some of those Zeros were flying without ammo.

It was a fun conversation with the old flying Ace. He enjoyed talking about his WW2 pilot years. I never saw him again after that. But I won't forget him telling me that some Japanese Zeros in the Great Marianas Turkey Shoot of 1944 didn't have bullets.

Traveling Germans

The highway to Sequoia National Park in California goes past Lake Kaweah. It is a winding, two lane highway that is busy with traffic much of the year. The campground at Lake Kaweah is an overnight stop for many of those park travelers. Germans far outnumber all other foreigners driving that roadway and camping at Kaweah.

During my five years working at Kaweah, I saw hundreds of German campers. There were days when Kaweah's campground had more Germans than Americans. I can't remember anything bad about a German traveler. They are wonderful people: prosperous, smart, honest, kind, generous, and they love to travel. They crisscross the United States more than Americans do. This story is a deserving tribute to all Germans everywhere. Tourists from Germany are top-of-the-line.

I still remember some German stories. Nudity in Germany is not considered a bad thing like it is here in America. There were times when American campers at Kaweah complained about nude Germans in the campground. I recall a couple of young German men who were traveling north from Kaweah on three-wheel bicycles. They were huffing and puffing peddling up those highway hills. What a long and difficult journey that would be; where is the fun in that? Once I was in the campground and a group of young Germans in a rented RV pulled up beside me. They were looking for a numbered campsite. I reached in my ranger truck and pulled out a cold twelve-pack of beer that I had just confiscated at the Slick Rock recreation area. I handed it to the Germans and they were puzzled. What were they supposed to do with it? I told them it was theirs. They were in disbelief. They travel all the way to California and get free cold beer.

Grand Jury

During my years of employment in California, I got summoned for jury selection numerous times but never served on a jury. After retirement I moved to Fresno, CA, and got a jury summons there. I showed up at the courthouse on a given day and time, along with about seventy-five other people. We all sat down in a courtroom in front of a lady judge, a lawyer, and a stenographer. The judge looked at her list of prospective jurors and began calling out names. Two dozen of us were reseated in a jury booth. We were each asked a few questions by the judge. Several people were dismissed and replaced by others. Within an hour the judge and lawyer had selected about two dozen jurors plus several alternates.

A head judge then came into the room and the lady assistant judge left. The head judge swore all of us in as jurors and told us what our job would be. We were now serving on a federal grand jury for a period of 12-18 months. We would meet in this courthouse every other Thursday morning to hear testimony for upcoming federal court cases. We would receive a salary plus travel expenses. Our purpose was to decide if evidence and testimony for upcoming federal court cases was legitimate, legal, and satisfactory. A majority yes vote, not a unanimous vote, was needed from the grand jury to allow a federal case to go to trial.

The grand jury I was part of represented a large district in California, so our jurors came from Sacramento all the way south to Los Angeles. Some were locals like me but others had to fly in and stay in motels and get taxied to the jury session.

Our first grand jury meeting took place a couple of weeks later. We were given security passes and seated in a room with a stenographer, a witness box, and an assistant district attorney. Witnesses were brought in and questioned by the attorney. Most of our sessions lasted 2-4 hours.

During the eighteen months that our grand jury met, we heard a wide variety of testimony and evidence. Our cases included dirty cops, fraud, illegal immigrants, child porn, terrorism, theft, assault, drugs, and so on. The most amazing case for me was a fraudster who bilked millions from an investment group by renting and selling property he didn't own.

It was a new experience for me and I learned much about the court system. I learned that court trials can be state or federal. State trials have twelve jurors who hear testimony and then decide on guilt or innocence. The jury verdict must be unanimous. A federal court case needs to meet certain legal criteria; then the evidence must first be presented to a grand jury. The grand jury decides by majority vote if the case can go forward to trial. A federal court case that goes to trial will have twelve jurors who consider the testimony and evidence. Their decision on guilt or innocence must be unanimous.

State trials encompass most of the arrest actions by law enforcement. Federal trials are generally for crimes involving inter-state actions and usually carry longer prison terms.

Jury Summons

After serving on a federal grand jury in Fresno, CA, for eighteen months, I was exempted from jury duty for the next three years. Three years passed and then came another jury summons in the mail. I went to the Fresno State courthouse where there was a long line of people. We were funneled into a very large room in front of a judge, a defendant, a prosecuting attorney, and three defense lawyers. We all took seats and the judge gave us the story.

There was a murder trial upcoming and it would get media attention because the prosecution was seeking the death penalty. One thousand people were being called for jury screening. The jury selection process would take several weeks; then the trial was expected to last another ninety days. Persons who needed to be excused from jury duty could fill out paperwork for that request.

Half the people in the room began filling out paperwork to be excused from the jury. The remaining half were given a questionnaire regarding opinions of the murder case and the death penalty. We were then told to go home and wait for instructions in the mail.

A few days later I got a letter telling me to be at the state courthouse on a given day and time for jury questioning. I showed up and joined a group of about eight people. One by one we were taken in front of the judge and lawyers and asked questions. Half of our group were dismissed; the other half were told to go home and wait for mail instructions. Several days later I headed to the state courthouse again. This time it was a courtroom session with the judge, defendant, and lawyers all present. The pool of prospective jurors had been reduced to about one hundred people.

Names were called and eighteen of us were seated in a jury booth. The judge explained that this jury selection process would continue until the lawyers were satisfied with the jury panel. The defense attorney stood up and went to the jury booth and spoke directly to one young female juror. In a loud voice he told her that his client wasn't planning to take the stand in his own defense but that shouldn't impact a juror's decision on guilt or innocence. The defense attorney wanted everyone in the room to hear what he was saying. I raised my hand and told him that if the defendant didn't testify in his own defense, I was leaning toward a guilty verdict. The defense lawyer smiled and said I could do that, but he wasn't pleased with what I'd said. The defense attorney spoke awhile longer and then the prosecuting attorney stood up. He told the jury panel that it is a privilege and an honor for citizens like us to be selected for jury service. I raised my hand and told him that I believe in the American court system but I didn't want to be a part of a three-month trial. He said he would consider that. Both lawyers talked awhile longer and then the judge called for a short recess. When we came back, the judge dismissed three jurors; my name was first. I asked the bailiff if I had to stay and he said no; I was done with this trial. I left and drove to the golf course.

I followed the results of that trial. The defendant was found guilty of murdering a senior husband and wife in a robbery. That part of the trial lasted only a couple of weeks. Then came the penalty phase of the trial which lasted much longer. Many witnesses came forth to argue for and against the death penalty. The final verdict from the jury was a life sentence without parole.

Superdome

In the late 1970s I was driving around the United States in a motorhome. Passing through Louisiana, I could see the Superdome in the distance. From the radio I learned that the New Orleans Saints would be playing a home game there, so I decided to go. It would be my first professional football game.

I aimed my RV toward the Superdome; the game was scheduled for the next day. The Superdome got bigger and bigger as I got closer and closer. I parked nearby and walked around. Superdome tours were available for a fee so I joined a tour group. A young lady gave our group a walking tour through the Superdome. It was an impressive structure.

The one thing I remember most about the Superdome tour was the hallways. Our group walked through long hallways from one place to another, and all the hallways had rounded edges and corners. There were no square corners or square edges on the floors or ceilings of any of the hallways. There was a reason for this I'd never heard before. People with claustrophobia can get frightened in a long hallway with square edges on the floor and ceiling. But if those square edges are rounded, the fear goes away. It sounds too simple, but evidently it is true.

The next day was game day so I parked my RV and walked to the Dome. I expected to buy a ticket at a box office but there were lots of people outside the Superdome waving tickets for sale. I bought one for seven dollars and went inside. The Saints were playing the Philadelphia Eagles that day and the Eagles had a winning team. The Saints had a poor record and a weak football team so the stadium was only half full. As I looked around, some of the fans had paper sacks over their heads with holes for eyes. They were showing their displeasure for the team and management.

The game turned out to be a good one. The Saints had a good quarterback, Archie Manning, and the Saints played tough that day. The Eagles won the contest but the score was close. The Saints fans were cheering hard in spite of their team's many losses.

That year the New Orleans Saints finished the season with a bad win/loss record, and it was the following football season when the Saints fans began wearing paper sacks over their heads En masse. During the football game I went to, there were a sprinkling of paper sacks visible in the crowd. But the next year, and I saw this on television, the stadium had thousands of Saints fans wearing paper sacks over their heads. They were making a statement to the owners.

Subsequent years saw the New Orleans Saints football team improve. They began contending for their division title. Next they were playing in post season playoffs. In 2010 the Saints took it all the way and won the Super Bowl.

The Takedown

I got off work that evening and stopped at a drugstore to buy a few things. I selected some store items and went to the counter to pay. Just then I heard a guy shout "There he goes." I looked around and saw a young man about seventeen years old trying to leave the store. A store employee, maybe twenty years old, was grabbing him. As the first guy struggled to get free, a second store employee about the same age ran to the action which was now happening outside. Two store employees were trying to hold on to a fellow who was attempting to run.

I assumed it was shoplifting. I had on my park ranger uniform so I handed my purchase items to the store clerk and told her to hold them for me. Then I ran outside to join the tussle. I grabbed the shoplifter around his chest, put one of my legs in front of his, and pushed. He went down on the ground with me on top. It was now three against one. The two store employees each kept a grip on one arm. I wrapped my two legs around one of the shoplifter's legs so he couldn't get up. He kept struggling but I told him it was no use. He wasn't going anywhere. Just relax.

The store clerk inside called the police and five minutes later a cop car arrived. The policeman could see what was happening as he walked toward us. He told us to let the guy up and I told him to cuff the guy first because he was a runner. When the handcuffs clicked on, then the store employees and I let go.

The two store workers started searching the runner's pockets and the cop told them that was his job. He pulled out a couple hundred dollars' worth of shoplifted items. After the runner was frisked clean, the cop hand-placed him in the police car and locked the door.

I went back inside the store to pay for my items. When the two workers came back in the store with the stolen stuff, I talked with them for a few minutes. The first guy to grab the shoplifter was small but he was a tough hombre. He told me he belonged to a neighborhood street gang. The second store employee was young and not very big either, but he wasn't afraid to scrap. Both of them were smaller than the shoplifter but they showed no fear going after the guy.

$75,000 Bail

It was late afternoon at Eastman Lake, CA. I was driving through the boat dock area on the day-use side of the lake. There were several vehicles in the parking lot and some fishermen on the shoreline. A fisherman walking across the parking lot waved at my ranger truck and showed me a broken window in his pickup. He pointed to a group of young men fishing and said they did it.

Just then a local Fish and Game Warden drove into the area so I flagged her over and asked her to stay. I knew her; she carried a gun and had arrest authority. I went down to the lake and told the group of fishermen, all about 20-25 years old, to come up to the parking lot. The Fish and Game Warden called on her radio for a police response to the scene.

Four young men walked up to the parking lot and I had them line up in front of the Game Warden. I looked for weapons while she told them to stay put. The fisherman with the broken window looked at the four and pointed to one of them. He said he believed that was the guy who had broken into his vehicle.

It took another ten minutes for the police to arrive. I showed them the broken car window and they put handcuffs on the fellow accused of breaking it. After checking his ID, they put him in the police car.

Then another man appeared and I never did figure out where he came from. He may have been hiding in a restroom or behind some bushes nearby. He walked across the parking lot and started to get in the vehicle belonging to the group of four young men. The fellow with the broken window saw him and told me that was the guy who had broken into his pickup; not the other guy. He was sure of it.

I went and told the policemen. They grabbed the fifth guy, put handcuffs on him, and released the other man. While checking the fifth guy's identification, it took a while because he didn't have an ID and he gave them a phony name and birthdate. After checking his tattoos, they finally figured out who he was. He was about twenty-five years old and had an outstanding warrant for $75,000. When the police told him what his real name was and how much bail money he was worth, he laughed and said "Only $75,000." He was wanted on a drug charge.

The police let the four men go and they drove off. The guy with the warrant was taken to jail. The fisherman was satisfied with the arrest. The Game Warden left to go patrolling elsewhere. And I was left wondering why the guilty man didn't wait for the cops to leave before showing himself. We didn't even know he was around until he walked across the parking lot.

Hollywood

Years ago I went to Hollywood for a look-see. I was living in Los Angeles that summer with a college friend. We took an afternoon drive to see Universal Studios.

Inside the headquarters at Universal Studios we looked around. Then we went outside and managed to sneak through a security gate leading to the movie sets. A uniformed security lady saw us wandering around and asked what we were doing there. We told her we were extras on one of the movie sets and pointed to some buildings in front of us. She looked around and said that was okay. Then she told us it was her job to check everybody because some people try to sneak in. We acted surprised and waved to her as she walked away.

A small building ahead of us showed some activity so we went inside. They were filming a movie titled "The Great Man's Whiskers". Actor Dennis Weaver was sitting in a chair looking like President Lincoln. A director operating a large movie camera was in charge. A girl about eight years old did a practice scene with Weaver and she was very good.

After watching the Lincoln skit, we left there and found another busy movie set in a different building. They were filming a scene for the television series "Dragnet". Jack Webb and Harry Morgan were sitting at a table interrogating a criminal. The criminal botched his lines on the first take and apologized several times. Webb told him it was okay; just relax. They did the scene again and it was a take. The criminal actor was relieved.

When we left that building, we saw George Hamilton, the actor, walk out of a small office. He stopped and did a relaxation pose, hands in his pockets, looking around. We walked over to him and said hi and shook his hand. We told him we recognized him; we were extras on one of the movie sets. He smiled and said hi. We waved at him as we walked off.

From there we headed back toward Universal headquarters, poking around here and there along the way. Eventually we made our way back to our car. We had seen a glimpse of Hollywood glitz.

We did learn one thing while inside the movie set area. Above the door to each movie set, both inside and outside, there is a red light. When that red light turns on, that means there is filming being done inside. The door is not to be opened: no noise, no disturbance. When that red light goes off, the film action has stopped and it is then safe to open the door and walk in or out.

Snakes - Part 1

There are four kinds of snakes in California that people will see. The green grass snake is harmless. The king snake looks poisonous and dangerous, with stripes of orange, purple, and yellow around it. King snakes eat small rodents and other snakes and are not poisonous. The gopher snake has coloring similar to a rattlesnake but its tail is pointed. The gopher snake has no rattles and is not poisonous. Rattlesnakes in California are smaller than those in Arizona and New Mexico. A four-foot rattlesnake in California is a large snake. Rattlesnakes shake their tail to give warning. A rattlesnake bite will result in pain but seldom do people die from a rattlesnake bite.

I saw lots of snakes during my years of working at California lakes. Occasionally a visitor would get bit by a rattler. When that happened, we called 911 and an ambulance medic would give the victim an anti-venom shot on site. Then the person would be transported to a hospital for a day or two there. Pain from a rattlesnake bite can last a week.

I got a radio call at Lake Kaweah one day about a rattlesnake in the campground. I went there and found about thirty people formed in a ring near a restroom. I knew what was in the middle. In the front row of spectators was a guy in a wheelchair, six feet away from a coiled rattlesnake. He didn't want to miss any of the action. I felt sorry for the snake.

I got a shovel from my ranger truck and went inside the circle of people. I explained to them that rattlesnakes are not aggressive; they only bite when they are frightened. The rattling of the tail is a warning to stay away. I told them park employees do not handle snakes and don't kill snakes unless necessary. If a rattlesnake is a threat to people, it will be dispatched. I then took my shovel and whacked the snake but the shovel bounced off. The snake made a flying leap at me so I swung the shovel again. This time the shovel cut the snake in half. I asked if anyone wanted the tail with rattles and a half dozen hands went up. I took the snake head with me and buried it elsewhere. Poison from a dead rattlesnake remains lethal for a year.

Another time while patrolling the Lake Kaweah campground, I saw a group of people huddled together in front of a restroom, looking at the ground. I went over and saw a king snake with the head of a live rattlesnake in its mouth. The king snake was about 2 ½ feet long and the rattlesnake was less than 2 feet. The king snake was getting itself positioned to eat the rattlesnake head first. The crowd of people didn't bother the king snake at all; it was working on a meal. I went and got my camera and snapped several pictures. One of those pictures was sent by Fish and Game to the California State Fair that year and it took second place in the Nature category.

A Boy Scout troop came to Eastman Lake for an overnight campout in the primitive campground. They encountered a three-foot rattlesnake near their campsite and called for a ranger. A student ranger went to the scene and being a nature-lover, he picked up the rattlesnake and moved it to the edge of the campground and let it go there. The scout leader wrote a letter of complaint to the Eastman office about the ranger releasing a rattlesnake in the campground where his scouts were tenting. The student ranger had violated both rattlesnake rules. He handled the snake and released it in an area where there were people. He lost his job.

There occurred a snake bite at Eastman Lake which was unusual. Camp hosts got a call about a snake bite in a group area. Rangers responded and learned that a person there had been bitten by a rattlesnake and was being driven to a hospital thirty miles away. When the victim arrived at the hospital, the emergency doctor confirmed the rattlesnake bite but there was no swelling. The victim felt no ill effects from the bite. The patient was kept under observation for awhile and it was determined to be a dry bite. The rattlesnake didn't inject any poison when the bite was made. Mature rattlesnakes can do this. They can regulate the amount of poison they inject with a bite, and they can bite without releasing any poison.

Snakes - Part 2

After my work shift ended at Eastman Lake, I paid a visit to a lady I knew in the campground. The sun was down so a lantern on the picnic table provided light. The weather was warm and I was dressed in shorts, with thongs on my feet. I got up from the table and walked to a nearby water spigot to get some water. Standing in front of the water spigot, I heard a faint noise and knew immediately what it was.

I couldn't see the rattlesnake in the darkness but I knew where it was. It was next to my left foot. I could tell how big it was by the sound of the rattle. And I knew it was coiled and ready to strike. Most importantly, I knew what to do in this situation.

I remained absolutely, perfectly motionless and told the lady to get her two dogs on a leash. Do it quick and don't ask why. Within a few seconds she had snapped her two golden retrievers to their leashes by the table. I then made a quick hop upward and backward toward the table. I felt no bite so I was safe. I told her "rattlesnake" and grabbed a flashlight from the table. Shining the light where I had been standing, a coiled rattler seventeen inches long didn't like the light and slithered down a hole several feet away.

I picked up a water hose, hooked it to the water spigot, and turned on the water. I put the hose in the hole and got a shovel and flashlight. Then I waited. It took several minutes for the hole to fill with water, then out came the snake. It didn't get far; I cut it in half with the shovel. The danger was over.

My lady friend was a little unnerved by all of this. She realized that she and her dogs weren't far from that rattlesnake in the dark. I looked around the campsite with the flashlight to make sure all was clear and safe. We were both relieved that nobody got bit. I was counting my blessings for not stepping on the snake. My bare legs were an open target and even small rattlesnakes have ample venom. I would have spent one or two days in a hospital and missed a week of work, feeling serious pain.

Bobby Beaver and the Roller Derby Queen

A student park ranger and I were working the weekend at Eastman Lake. His parents were camping in the campground so he volunteered to do a program that evening in the amphitheater. He wanted to do something extra for his folks.

He and I went to the primitive campground where a Boy Scout troop was camping. We told them we needed their help. There would be a program that evening in the campground and we needed a Bobby Beaver. They told us they had the perfect volunteer for the job. They wouldn't miss the program for anything.

The student ranger and I went to the office and got the Bobby Beaver suit. We left it with the scouts and told them when the program would start. Then we advertised the show to all campers.

That evening at showtime the scouts showed up at the amphitheater with a scout leader dressed in the Bobby Beaver suit. Other campers were there, including the parents of the student ranger. The student ranger took the stage with Bobby Beaver and explained why Bobby was there. Bobby is a reminder for people to be safe around the water.

Then another scout leader went on stage and played his guitar to the tune "You Are My Sunshine". But the scouts changed the lyrics to "You Are Our Bobby" and sang new Bobby Beaver words with the song. When the scouts finished their song, the student ranger then invited volunteers from the audience to come on stage and sing. A little girl five years old walked up on stage and began singing "He's Got the Whole World in His Hands". She was so good that by the second verse, everybody in the audience was standing, clapping their hands in rhythm, and singing along with her. She was a sensation and the show was very entertaining.

Afterward I visited the scouts and congratulated them. I talked to the scout leader who had played Bobby Beaver. He introduced me to his girlfriend and said she knew plants. She could do a campground program about plants. We set it up for the following weekend. He and his scouts and his girlfriend camped overnight the next weekend and she did a campground program about plants.

After that show I visited them and learned that the girlfriend not only knew about plants, she also knew about roller skating. She belonged to a Fresno roller derby team. I'd never seen a roller derby contest except on television so I quizzed her about it: when and where? I wanted to see her team skate. She gave me a date, time, and location where her team would be scrimmaging against another female roller derby team.

I told some of my friends about it, including the campground hosts and some park volunteers. On match day we had two carloads of people headed to Fresno to see the roller derby action. We found the rink in the downtown area and went inside. The skaters showed up and began warming up. We in the audience were amazed at how well and fast those ladies could skate. Each team had a coach and the teams had sponsor support. The skaters started scrimmaging, with one referee present. The skaters moved around the oval rink doing jamming, blocking, passing, and breakaways. It was fun to watch and something I still remember. Those ladies were as skilled on roller skates as hockey players are on ice.

Helicopter Medical

I hadn't been there five minutes when I saw it happen. I parked my ranger truck at the day-use parking lot and scanned the boats on the lake. A boat with several young men on board was pulling a skier. I knew the boat and the two brothers who owned it. The skier did a mid-air turnaround and took a hard splash. When he surfaced, I heard him yell in a loud voice to the boat.

Next, the boat came charging toward the dock in my direction. A fellow jumped out of the boat onto the dock and ran toward me waving his hand. He told me the skier had a serious leg injury and was requesting a helicopter medical team right away. I knew who the injured man was. He was one of the two brothers who owned the boat and he knew about helicopters. He was currently in training to become a helicopter pilot himself.

I called on my radio to police dispatch and told them a water skier was down with a serious leg injury. The skier was requesting a medical helicopter to the Eastman Lake day-use dock ASAP. While I made the radio call, the boat headed back out to pick up the injured skier in the water. It took awhile for the boaters to get the victim loaded into the boat. Then came the sound of a helicopter approaching as the boat returned to the dock.

I called for ranger support as the chopper began descending toward the parking lot. One ranger kept vehicle traffic out of the parking area. Another ranger did foot patrol to keep onlookers away from the helicopter, with blades still turning. An ambulance arrived and drove directly to the boat at the dock. Medical people carefully put the injured skier on a stretcher and drove him to the helicopter. The victim and several medics were then transferred inside the helicopter whereupon it lifted off for Fresno.

I talked to the boaters and they said the bone break was ugly, with ripped skin and muscle tissue. In the weeks ahead, I saw the boat at the lake and asked about the injured brother. I was told the helicopter flying lessons had been put on hold and the healing process was very slow. In the end it took a year for the man's leg to heal and the helicopter training to resume.

Life After Burial

I met a lady when I was working on a riverboat. She was the cook; a nice lady and we became friends. She was mid-thirties and Hispanic. We were talking about paranormal stuff and she told me a story that sounded crazy. After I heard her story, I didn't know what to think. I didn't believe it but she had no reason to lie to me. The best I could do was believe that it may have happened.

She told me her grandmother had died. The family dressed the body in nice clothes, put some favorite jewelry on her, and had an open-casket ceremony in a chapel. The coffin was then buried, and that night some grave robbers dug up the casket to remove the jewelry. The lady was still alive; she had awakened and was clawing her fingernails into the top of the casket. The grave robbers were frightened off and the grandmother survived.

There are holes in this story but I didn't ask many questions after I heard it. I should have asked if the burial happened in Mexico. I have difficulty seeing something like this happening in the United States unless it was many, many years ago. Now there are laws and coroners and funeral homes that would make this kind of mistake nearly impossible.

But the cook's story didn't end there. She went on to say that her grandmother lived on for a while after. When she died again, this time the family waited several days to make sure she was really dead. Then they cleaned and dressed the body and had a chapel ceremony with an open casket. During that ceremony, with a priest present, a white light from above began to glow upon the lady in the casket. The priest and everyone present could see a column of white light streaming down through the ceiling, surrounding the body. The priest knelt down on the floor and clasped his hands in amazement. The white light continued as people filed past the open casket. The cook telling me this story said the light was so prominent on the face that she could see fine hairs around the lips. Everyone present took this as a heavenly sign.

The lady was buried again and this time with no problems. The gravesite wasn't disturbed. The family felt peace that their grandmother must be in heaven. The white-light phenomenon was a pleasant memory for all of them.

The second part of this story I can visualize. Most people have heard of a white-light phenomenon, whether in scripture or elsewhere. But the first part of the story is more difficult to imagine or accept, until you watch the television program "Antiques Roadshow UK Season 23 Episode 4". That show has a story about a lady who died of black plague in the 1700s. She was buried in a tomb with a gold ring on her finger that was so tight, people couldn't remove it. After her burial, the butler went into the tomb and cut off her finger to get the gold ring. She came to life and lived many years after that. She gave birth to two children after her rebirth from the tomb. After hearing that Roadshow story, I now believe that the first part of this grandma tale is possible. The grandmother may have awakened in the coffin and lived on after the robbers dug her up.

The Intruder

I was in Las Vegas, parked in my motorhome behind a grocery mall. It was evening and I had a small light on above my kitchen sink. I was sitting in the rear of my RV watching television when I heard the front door handle click open. I turned my head to see a large fellow stepping up into my RV. Seeing the man enter my motorhome blocked out all my fears. I felt no fear or mercy when I stood up and grabbed a sharp knife from the dish tray. Within seconds I had his shirt gripped at the neck and the knife at his throat. He knew he'd made a mistake and then he morphed into a marshmallow. All he could do was whimper and cry over and over that he only wanted to sleep on the floor. He needed a place to sleep.

I knew he was lying. He looked like a homeless guy, a thief rather than a fighter. I put my knife down and told him to have a seat. I asked when he last had a meal and was he hungry? He said he would like some food. So I turned around and reached into an upper cabinet, pulled out my travel checks and detached one. Then I took my car keys and wallet and told the guy to stay put. I would go buy some groceries and fix him a meal.

I bought some food in the store and fixed a meal for both of us. Then I told him he could sleep on the floor for a night if he wanted. It was chilly weather outside. He thanked me for the meal and said he would like to sleep on the floor. The next morning he left and so did I.

It was a couple of weeks later when I noticed some of my travel checks were missing. The homeless fellow had seen me get the travel checks, and when he detached several of them, he didn't take them from the top. He took several in the middle so nobody would notice.

I had to call a bank to report the theft and the check company sent me a refund in the mail.

Wanted

Years ago I was in my motorhome parked somewhere in the Southwest U.S. It was summer and relatively hot. My RV was the only vehicle in a small rest area with restrooms and picnic tables. Nothing was happening until a fellow showed up on foot. I watched him for a while. He had no car or backpack. He was about age thirty, looking tired and dirty, sitting at one of the tables.

After a time I went outside and said hi to him. He was friendly. I asked about his car and he said he had no car. He'd been walking and was tired. I invited him into my motorhome to get him a drink. I asked if he needed food and he said he hadn't eaten for a while. I reached into my refrigerator and took out a big fat carrot. I told him to go outside and munch on the carrot. I would drive to a small town nearby and buy some groceries. Then I would return and cook a meal for both of us. That sounded like a good plan to him.

So I did that. When I got back, he was still munching on the big carrot. I fixed us a meal and quizzed him about where he was headed? Why was he walking? His story turned out ugly. The police had just identified and impounded his car at a truck stop a few miles away and they were looking for the owner. He was wanted by the law and everything he owned was in his car. He now had nothing but the dirty clothes he was wearing. He was on foot and on the run and didn't want to go to jail.

We finished the meal and he went to the restroom and washed himself and his clothes as best he could. He hung his clothes out to dry and I loaned him some clothes to wear. He didn't seem like a threat to me; he was cordial and appreciated my help. I told him he could sleep on the floor of my RV for the night if he wanted.

The next morning I fixed breakfast for us and then drove up the road a few miles to a truck weigh station that I'd seen. There he could hitch a ride with a trucker. I gave him a five-dollar bill and wished him luck. He thanked me again for my help. I drove off knowing that fellow was facing a tough future.

Big Buck and Drummers

Three Rivers is a small city just above Lake Kaweah in the central California Valley. It's a scenic town in a scenic area. I worked at Lake Kaweah for five years so I got to know the city. Residents of Three Rivers are good people: progressive, educated, prosperous, free thinkers, nature lovers.

There is an area along the edge of the city where deer like to graze on the grass. A big buck deer became a regular visitor to that grassy area. Many townspeople knew about the big buck and had seen it. It became a Three Rivers icon because of its size and antlers.

A resident living in that area realized he could bag an easy trophy deer if he bought a hunting license, so he applied for and received a deer tag from the California Department of Fish and Game. One day when the big buck came strolling past his property, he went out on his back porch with his rifle and shot it.

The city exploded with rage. Letters to the Editor poured in to the local newspaper for weeks and weeks. City residents felt the pain of what had happened to their beloved trophy buck, and they knew who was responsible. It took a long time for the city to forget about that gunshot.

I got to know some of the Three Rivers residents. One fellow was a progressive, educated free thinker who built an art gallery there. His building design was very unique: the walls could be turned out from the inside for easy access. He had lots of local artwork on display and for sale in his gallery.

He asked me one day if his drumming group could meet on Fire Island in the middle of Lake Kaweah. He went on to explain that every week on a certain day, a Three Rivers drum group would meet somewhere for a drumming session. Anybody could come and either watch or participate. I told the fellow I didn't see why his group couldn't get together on an island in Lake Kaweah. He asked if I knew a way to get the people out to the island, maybe twenty people. I told him I would check around and get back to him.

I asked some Kaweah house boaters and one man agreed to transport the drummers. I called the Three Rivers fellow and told him transportation was available. On a given day and time about twenty people from Three Rivers gathered at a Kaweah boat dock, and I was among them. I wanted to see what this drumming thing was all about.

The houseboat arrived and everybody got on board. The house boater chugged out to Fire Island and dropped us off, with instructions to return in one hour. Then the drumming began. Half the people had drums or percussion instruments of some kind. The other half were like me, just there for the entertainment. The drumming went on for forty-five minutes and then the houseboat returned. Everybody reboarded the vessel for the return trip.

The next day at work I told my co-workers I'd been out on Fire Island the previous evening with drummers from Three Rivers. The senior ranger heard me and asked what it was all about. I explained that a group of people from Three Rivers meet weekly at different locations for drumming sessions. He asked if it sounded good and I told him no. It sounded like excess noise to me. The Kaweah manager asked me about the Three Rivers drummers; what kind of people were they? I told him they weren't mainstream.

Meth Lab

At Lake Kaweah, when I worked there, I met and got to know a lot of people. One character that I became friends with knew a lot of bad guys in the area. He was an ex-con. I asked him one day about a suspicious vehicle and described it. He said he knew the car and the owner. He told me where the owner lived and that he was fencing stolen property from his home. I called that information in to the police and they busted the guy several weeks later.

Not long after that, there was a drug bust across the highway from Lake Kaweah. A meth operation was uncovered and shut down. When I saw my character friend again, I told him about the drug bust. He informed me that there was a wooden shed just north of Lake Kaweah where meth was being cooked. Days later I happened to meet and talk with a lake visitor who said he lived just north of the lake. I asked if he knew anything about a wooden shed in that area and he said he did; he could see it from his residence. I told him that shed was reportedly being used to cook meth. He thought for a minute and said he did see vehicles there from time to time.

That homeowner made contact with the Three Rivers deputy when he saw him in town. They discussed the meth shed and what could be done. A couple of weeks later I was patrolling Lake Kaweah and heard a radio call from the Three Rivers deputy to the Kaweah contract deputy. Be on the lookout for a certain vehicle. Fifteen minutes later I drove past a Kaweah recreation area and saw two sheriff deputies putting handcuffs on a big fellow next to his car.

The Kaweah deputy filled me in later on details. When he got the BOL radio call, he was driving the highway beside the lake. He looked up and there in front of him was the BOL vehicle. All he had to do was flash his lights and call the Three Rivers deputy. They found drugs and cash in the car and took the guy to jail. That vehicle had been seen at the wooden shed north of the lake.

One other meth-lab story comes from Eastman Lake. An Eastman volunteer stopped at the office one day and reported what looked like a drug dump site. I drove to the park entrance and found some large buckets of clear liquid sitting alongside the road. There were also buckets of other waste products, all of which looked drug related. We called the police and they called for a Hazmat specialist to confirm and clean up the site.

I talked with the Hazmat fellow when he was cleaning the site. He said this kind of drug waste dumping is common practice. Drug labs need to get rid of dangerous waste products so they let law enforcement do it for them. They place their toxic chemicals where law enforcement can find it and dispose of it. The Hazmat guy told me that most dump sites are located within five miles of where the meth was made. He estimated the street value of the meth produced from the Eastman Lake dump site at a quarter million dollars.

Heat Exhaustion

One afternoon I stopped at a recreation area at Lake Kaweah to do some ranger patrol on foot. In the parking lot a young man hurried over to me and said there was something wrong with his wife. Could I help her? I walked with him to where she was sitting on a blanket and she looked like a rag doll. I knew immediately what the problem was. The temperature was 90 degrees and this lady was suffering from heat exhaustion.

I grabbed one of her arms and told the husband to grab the other arm. We needed to get her to his car as quickly as possible. She was limp as we walked/carried her to the car. He opened the car door and we set her in the passenger seat. I tilted the seat back and told him to have her drink some water or liquid. She needed to drink a lot of water. As she drank, I told him she was in a state of heat exhaustion. She needed to be cooled down and get fluids in her body. Drinking water was the most important thing for her to do. As long as she had liquids in her body, she would be okay and recover fine. There would be no harm or danger to her if she kept drinking liquids. Get her home, put her in bed, and keep liquids in her.

He thanked me and drove away. A week later he came to the Kaweah office and thanked the ranger staff for helping his wife. She was fine and fully recovered from her spell of heat exhaustion.

Symptoms of heat exhaustion and heat stroke are easy to recognize. Heat exhaustion is the first stage of a body getting overheated, which brings on heavy perspiration, weakness, and dizziness. The remedy is to get out of the heat and drink plenty of liquids.

Heat stroke is an advanced stage of heat exhaustion and very serious. When the body loses its fluids and can no longer perspire, the body temperature rises. Perspiration is the body's way of cooling itself. A person suffering from heat stroke needs to drink water or liquids immediately to restart the perspiration process. Heat stroke can bring death in a short time.

Flood Water

I worked for the federal government in California for twenty years and didn't see one single manager or senior ranger who could spend taxpayer dollars wisely. At Eastman Lake, the managers used summer seasonal workers for silly nature projects that wasted time, money, and manpower. At Lake Kaweah, the management and senior ranger team had trees and vegetation planted along the river above the lake to enhance the river beauty. I was tasked with writing a brochure showing the different plants and trees along that river trail. I spent time doing that and the brochure was typed, pictured, and printed at the Sacramento District office.

A couple of years after I began working at Kaweah, there came a warm rain from the south in February. Sacramento Corps District saw the weather forecast and lowered all the central California Corps lakes to minimum pool. When the warm rain moved across central California, the snow melt came rushing down the foothills. Kaweah drains a large area of foothills and the lake began to rise even with a maximum release of water from the dam. It turned out to be a flood seen once every fifty years. Water rushing down the Kaweah river through the city of Three Rivers tore out a steel/concrete bridge. The flow rate reached 70,000 cubic feet of water per second.

Every plant and tree between Three Rivers and Lake Kaweah, a distance of ten miles, was ripped out and pushed into the lake. All the floating trees, plants, and refuse along the river were pushed to the dam. The Kaweah Marina broke loose with many of the houseboats sent floating. The water release at Kaweah dam was kept at maximum flow and still the lake level rose to the dam overflow. The rush of floodwater continued for a week.

When it was over, Kaweah was a mess. It took months for the Kaweah maintenance crew to clean the trees, vegetation, and trash from the front of the dam. It took time to repair the marina and refasten it to the shore. The river shoreline from Lake Kaweah to Three Rivers was sterile of vegetation. Nothing was left.

Managers at Lake Kaweah had forgotten there was a reason why the river between Three Rivers and the lake didn't have lots of trees and vegetation to look at. They forgot about Mother Nature.

Las Vegas

Las Vegas is a fun city, if you can keep from losing your shirt at the gaming tables and slot machines. I've seen Vegas many times and I would guess that 85% of my trips there end up with gambling losses. But I bet low so my gambling losses are low. I have fun playing the slot machines knowing that I'm helping to fuel the city's economy.

I've been inside most of the casinos in Las Vegas. The south half of Las Vegas Boulevard has the big fancy casinos. The Venetian is plush. The Bellagio has an outdoor water show. Excalibur has reasonable room rates during the weekdays. The Stratosphere in the center of town has a nice view from the top. Visitors staying at the Stratosphere can ride the elevator to the top for free; others pay a modest fee. Numerous Station Casinos, all large and very nice, are spread around the city. Vegas has casinos scattered everywhere.

My favorite hangout in Las Vegas is Fremont Street. It's the city's old gambling center, now remodeled for foot traffic. The Four Queens Casino there has reasonable room rates on weekdays with no resort fee surcharge. Activity on Fremont Street includes restaurants, casinos, evening outdoor bands, zip line, overhead light shows, and lots of strange people. I've been to Fremont Street on Halloween several times which is wild and crazy.

A lady friend and I both received a free slot-tournament coupon in the mail from The Orleans Casino so we went. When we got there, we were told that only one person per room could play in the tournament. So I played, with the agreement that if I won anything, we would split the winnings. The tournament had two sessions the same day, and both my scores were good. That evening upon returning to The Orleans, we checked the tournament winner's list. My name was on top. We split the $2500 cash prize for first place, and that's the only slot tourney I've ever won.

One trip to Las Vegas, my lady friend brought her daughter and granddaughter. We stayed on Fremont Street and did some gambling and sight-seeing that evening. The next day, while driving Las Vegas Boulevard, we were talking about the freaky people on Fremont Street. Who was the freakiest? While stopped at a stop light, we looked over and saw a short fellow walking along a sidewalk scratching himself. He was scratching all around his body, here and there, over and over, like druggies do. We voted him the freakiest and called him "bug boy".

Later that same day we were all in the car; I was driving a side street and paying attention to street signs. The granddaughter in the backseat said "Does that lady have any clothes on?" I looked to my left and saw a young lady walking out of what looked like a sleezy dance bar, and she was naked as a jaybird. She looked Hispanic, maybe twenty-five years old, medium height, slender body, small breasts. She wasn't bad looking but she needed a bath.

She was walking toward a fellow who was pulling a large plastic garbage can with wheels along the sidewalk. He looked like a homeless guy, and he looked back at the naked lady only once. Then he kept walking along the sidewalk pulling the big garbage can. She was pointing at him, telling him to bring that garbage can back. He didn't pay any attention to her; he kept on pulling the garbage can.

I was driving slowly, looking over my shoulder to watch this scene play out. She was catching up to him on the sidewalk, but some cars behind me forced me onward. Driving slowly, I was looking in the mirror and the three ladies in my car were all looking back. But we couldn't see who ended up with the garbage can.

The Memorial

It was October, 2017, when a mass shooting happened in Las Vegas. A lone gunman in the Mandalay Bay Hotel opened fire on a crowd of people below who were listening to a concert. More than fifty people were killed and hundreds were wounded.

I took a trip to Vegas several weeks later with a lady and we drove past the concert area and Mandalay Bay. Down the street, at the south end of Las Vegas Boulevard, a memorial had been set up. A steady stream of Vegas visitors were walking to and from that memorial. I parked nearby and we walked there. The memorial was a long, curved row of small white crosses with names and pictures of the shooting victims. All of the crosses were covered with beads, necklaces, flowers, cards, and letters. Visitors could feel the grief for those innocent people killed.

One visitor there I took notice of. She was about fifty years old, walking slowly among the white crosses, quietly sobbing. Her arm and upper chest were heavily bandaged, with one arm in a sling. As she moved from cross to cross, her hand covered her mouth as she wept. Watching her, I could think only one thing. She was one of the shooting victims.

After that tragedy, all of the large Station Casinos across the city offered free "Vegas Strong" t-shirts to rewards club members. I still have mine.

Reno, Pahrump, Laughlin

I don't do long distance driving anymore, but ten years ago I was taking trips to Las Vegas, Reno, Pahrump, and Laughlin.

Reno's economy took a serious hit from the real estate and banking bust of 2007/08. Some of the major casinos there closed and the city had many unemployed and homeless people. Five years later Reno looked better and was pushing forward, getting back on its feet. The Sands Casino and Circus Circus Casino have reasonable room rates on weekdays. In the center of Reno are three large casinos: Circus Circus, Silver Legacy, and Eldorado. These three casinos are connected and now under a single ownership. Numerous smaller casinos are spread around the city.

A lady friend and I occasionally visited Pahrump, Nevada, because we knew folks living there. The highway from California to Pahrump turns onto highway 127, and part of that drive is very scenic. It has an unusual moonscape look. There are four or five small casinos in Pahrump. Outside of town about ten miles are two legal brothels. One was offering free tours so my lady friend and I asked for a tour. The brothel had a meal menu and a sex menu. A thirty-year-old escort gave us a tour and offered to do a threesome with us. I didn't ask for a price. She told us that sex prices were flexible and bargained in the rooms, not from the menu. In the main building were rooms for short-time fun. All the rooms were nice and clean. Out back there were bungalows for overnight fun. The madam let us know that the tour was free but tips were appreciated, so I gave our escort a $5 tip.

Laughlin, Nevada, became a busy gambling hub after a bridge was built there connecting Arizona to Nevada. There are a number of small but nice casinos on the Nevada side. For sightseeing, a person can drive to Oatman, Arizona, not far away and see the wild donkeys there. Visitors bring carrots to feed the donkeys that roam through the town. Further up the highway is Lake Havasu City which now has the real London Bridge. The London Bridge was purchased by Lake Havasu City and shipped across the ocean in pieces, then reassembled at Lake Havasu. It is an engineering marvel.

MH Fire

I was working in New Mexico at the time, middle-aged and living in my motorhome. My RV was old but I did annual maintenance on it to keep it operational. My finances were lean so I depended heavily on my RV for living quarters and transportation. Daily I did inspections inside and outside on my motorhome, looking for any problems.

One afternoon I drove to my work site and shut the engine off. I stepped outside to walk around the vehicle and do a visual check like I often did. In front of my motorhome I saw a wisp of smoke, so I looked through the front grill into the engine compartment. A small flame had started where a hot battery wire was touching some oil and grease. Immediately my adrenaline went to full throttle because I knew this small fire would be out of control within minutes.

The panic and fear I felt as I ran back inside my motorhome was probably the most I've ever experienced in my entire life. I knew that my RV and everything I owned would burn to the ground within twenty minutes if I didn't act quickly. I was shaking from panic as I raised the inside cover over my engine. The flames were growing because of the oil and grease there. With difficulty, I managed to prop up my engine hood cover while trying to stay calm. I was talking to myself, telling myself to stay calm and stay in control. I was still shaking when I headed for my fire extinguisher. From a closet I grabbed my extinguisher but I had to figure out how to make it work. My thinking was confused because of my panic. I managed to pull the safety pin and then went back to the fire. Flames were now twelve inches high as I aimed the nozzle of the extinguisher and pulled the trigger. Out came a blast of white powder which extinguished the flames. I gave the area another blast of powder just to be sure. The fire was done. The engine was a mess but my panic and thinking began to settle down. The crisis was over.

I surveyed the engine compartment. The fire had started on the compartment wall and didn't reach the engine so the

133

motorhome engine wasn't damaged. That was a huge relief. I spent some time cleaning around the engine, washing and wiping away all the powder and grease. Then I covered the bare battery wire. I turned the engine on and it was operational again. I counted my lucky stars.

Luck was with me that day. If the engine had been damaged, I didn't have enough money to replace it. And if my motorhome had burned, I would have lost my transportation, my living quarters, and everything I owned. I don't know what I would have done. That walk-around inspection, plus the fact that I had a fire extinguisher, saved my bacon that day.

Wheelchair Fisherman

I was operating a patrol boat on Eastman Lake one afternoon, looking for any problems. At the base of the dam were two men fishing from the shore. One I knew; the other was fishing from a wheelchair. The trail leading down to the lake is a steep and lengthy down slope. I wondered how the wheelchair fisherman had gotten there and how he would get back home.

After an hour on the lake, I pulled the boat off the water and parked it at the office. Then I got a ranger truck and patrolled both sides of the lake. Before ending my work shift, I checked on the two fishermen at the dam. They were still there so I walked the trail down to where they were fishing.

One of the fishermen I knew well. He was a muscular guy and said he carried his paraplegic friend down to the shoreline to fish. I asked how he intended to get his friend back up the hill and he said he would carry him. The two said they were about ready to leave so maybe I could help. Could I pull the wheelchair and carry a bucket of fishing gear up the hill for them?

So here's the scenario. The paraplegic guy weighs about 200 pounds. My friend weighs about 240 pounds and is built like a pro wrestler. I'm going to follow him up the hill pulling a lightweight wheelchair and carrying a plastic five-gallon bucket with fishing poles and fishing gear in it.

The muscled guy lifted up his disabled friend and slung him over his head onto his back, then started stepping up the hill. I'm watching him carry this heavy load up a long, steep slope. I'm struggling behind him, pulling a wheelchair and carrying the bucket. He doesn't stop. It takes him five minutes to reach the top whereupon he turns around and waits for me. I'm not far behind but I am tired. My friend then puts his friend in the wheelchair and wheels him to the parking lot. I follow with the bucket and fishing gear and poles.

I don't think I'll ever forget seeing that guy hike up that steep incline with 200 pounds on his back. His leg muscles and arm

135

muscles looked like a pro wrestler in action. That's how strong he was. It was all I could do to climb the hill pulling a lightweight wheelchair and carrying a bucket. At the top, my friend did admit that he was tired.

Covid

The mobile home park where I currently reside is seniors only, so when coronavirus went global, residents here were looking for a vaccination ASAP. Several residents in our park died from covid before vaccinations were approved.

When covid vaccinations did become available, most of the residents here got the shot soon, and followed up with booster shots. But not everybody. A small percentage of people in our park didn't trust the vaccine because it was new. The park manager and his wife chose not to get vaccinated. They both worked in the office and both of them came down with coronavirus. The park manager was overweight and not in good health to begin with. They both ended up in the hospital. She got better and went back home, but he didn't improve. A week later he was placed on a ventilator, and soon after he died.

So our mobile park now has a new manager. Most of the seniors and staff here have had the first covid shot and at least one booster shot. I've gotten the first shot and three boosters since. Why somebody would choose not to get a free covid immunization shot makes no sense.

I played golf recently with a retired fellow. He told me that he and his wife had gone to a coronavirus party a year earlier. Only two people at the party were not vaccinated, he and his wife. They were afraid of the vaccine. Both of them got coronavirus after the party and both went to the hospital. It took him a month to recover but he pulled through. Before his wife died, she confided to him that maybe they should have gotten vaccinated.

Fort Knox

Long ago I visited the U.S. Mint in Washington, D.C., as part of a tour group. A guide led us through parts of the Mint and then up a flight of stairs. At the second level we were able to look down on the first floor where employees were working. We could see large sheets of paper money being cut into bills. Workers were inspecting sheets of money for defects. The employees below paid no attention to visitors above them because they were accustomed to being observed by tour groups.

After that trip to D.C., I was driving through Kentucky and noticed that Fort Knox wasn't far away. I decided to go there and tour the U.S. Gold Depository. I drove to the military base there and had no problem getting in. I asked a soldier at the entrance gate about the Depository and he gave me directions. A short drive took me to the Depository which was a large white building made of stone. Surrounding the building was a tall metal fence with a locked gate. I looked around for a parking area but couldn't see one.

Shutting off my engine, I stepped out of my motorhome and walked around, looking for visitor parking or another entrance. Then I heard a voice. I couldn't see anyone but on top of the fence gate was a metal speaker. I approached the speaker and said I wanted to take a tour of the Gold Depository. The speaker didn't reply. After a few more minutes of scouting around, I concluded that tours weren't available for visitors. The front gate was as close as I would get to the gold bullion.

Many years later, I watched a television news documentary about the Fort Knox Gold Depository. Some important U.S. dignitaries and politicians wanted access inside the Depository to see if gold was there in sufficient quantity. It didn't happen. Important as they were, those dignitaries were not able to get inside. The gist of the show was that outsiders are not allowed entrance into the Depository. The gold bars there are not for viewing and don't get moved around.

Murderers

I was in my late twenties when I met Popeye. We were
both parked in a free camping area in one of the eastern states. I
was traveling in a motorhome and he had a pickup camper. He was
a friendly fellow, maybe fifty-five years old, and we did some
chatting. He looked like the cartoon character Popeye the Sailor
Man and could do an impersonation of Popeye singing with a pipe
in his mouth.

Popeye wore a large belt buckle that had a small derringer
pistol in it. I asked if it was real and he slipped it out and showed
me it was loaded. He said he used it once; coming out of a grocery
market he found a man trying to open his car trunk. When he
asked the guy what he was doing, the robber saw the derringer
pointed at him and ran away.

Popeye told me some gun stories; he knew about guns. He
was on a submarine during World War 2 and the sub captain was
aggressive. He would sometimes surface the submarine at night
and send sailors ashore in a rubber raft to scout Japanese-held
islands. On one of those recon missions, Popeye and his mates
found an underground bunker where Japanese soldiers were
having a party. They dropped several grenades into the bunker and
then ran for the beach. A Japanese soldier hiding in the dark near
the beach stepped out and stabbed Popeye with a gun bayonet. An
American soldier following behind Popeye shot the Jap and helped
Popeye get back to the sub. It took a long time for that bayonet
wound to heal.

After the war, Popeye took up residence in the eastern U.S.
He was parked one evening in a pickup camper behind a freeway
rest area, not far from his hometown. He was sitting in his camper
drinking coffee in the dark, but he could see outside because of a
light at the restroom. Two men showed up at the rest area and
went in the restroom. When they came out, they stood looking at
Popeye's vehicle. They talked quietly and then began walking
slowly toward his camper.

Popeye could see the men through his curtains. Reaching into a drawer, he pulled out his pistol and checked it for ammunition. He thought his door was locked but he heard the door knob begin to turn. Suddenly the door burst open and a big guy stepped up into his camper, shouting "Okay old man, come out of there!" Popeye pointed the pistol at the man's belly and pulled the trigger. The gun was loaded with hollow-point shells, so when the bullet hit the intruder, it exploded. The man flew backwards out of the camper onto the pavement.

The fellow behind the intruder froze for several seconds. He was looking at his pal lying on the blacktop with a big hole in his stomach. When he regained his senses, he looked up and saw Popeye standing in the doorway with a pistol in his hand. He turned and ran. Popeye said he fired at the man running away, but the first bullet hit something metal inside the guy's backpack. So he fired again and the man went down. Now there were two dead men lying on the pavement behind the highway restrooms. Not wanting to face the police, Popeye closed his camper door, turned on his engine, and drove away.

Popeye didn't live far away so he drove home. The next day the news was all about the double murder at the rest area. A friend of Popeye's worked for law enforcement and it was days later when they saw each other. The friend began telling Popeye the latest news about the shooting and said the police had finally figured out who the two dead men were. They were wanted criminals, on the run from the New England area where they had killed several people.

After hearing that the two dead men were wanted murderers, Popeye confided to his friend that he knew who killed the bad guys. It was a case of self-defense. If the police promised not to prosecute, the shooter would come forth and tell the whole story.

The law-enforcement friend took that offer to the police department and they agreed. They had no interest in bringing charges against the shooter and wanted to close the case. For them it was thumbs up. They wanted to hear the story.

So Popeye went to the police station with his friend and replayed for them what happened. The case was closed and no tears were shed.

More Snakes and Animals

I was patrolling the Eastman Lake campground one day and came across a large king snake. There were numerous campers in that area so I decided to move the snake out of the campground. I grabbed it and headed back toward my ranger truck. Some campers saw the snake wiggling in my hand so they came over for a look. I showed them the colored snake, about three feet long, and explained that king snakes are not poisonous. Then more campers came over to see the big snake. Within a few minutes I was surrounded by twenty campers. So I did a snake presentation for the group before relocating it elsewhere.

Another time in the Eastman campground I caught a gopher snake about two and a half feet long. There was a cloth sack in my ranger truck so I put the snake in the sack. Driving through the campground, I stopped to chat with a group of adults and kids and took the cloth sack with me. When I reached into the sack and pulled out the snake, all the kids backed up five feet. I explained to the group that the gopher snake has a brown color similar to a rattlesnake but it is harmless. I showed them the pointed tail which identifies the gopher snake.

The kids began moving closer to get a better view so I held the snake out and handed it to the oldest girl there. She took the snake and now all the kids are crowding around her, wanting to see and touch. So, with the parents there, I gave the group of kids a mission. They were to take the snake and show it to all the campers and explain the difference between a gopher snake and a rattlesnake. When they were done, they were to let the snake loose outside the campground.

So off they went. All the kids started going from campsite to campsite, doing a show-and-tell with the gopher snake. When they finished, they let the snake go.

Another afternoon I saw some Boy Scouts in the Eastman campground so I stopped. I knew the scout leader who was cooking. He asked me if I wanted a taste of rattlesnake meat. I'd never eaten rattlesnake before so I gave it a try. It was good; it ooked and tasted like chicken. The rattlesnake was big but it didn't have enough meat to fill one person, so we all got just a sample portion.

The manager at Eastman Lake told a funny story about a friend who visited his family. She was a foreigner from Scandanavia. The manager and his wife did some home cooking for their guest that evening. They prepared an assortment of different foods including some cooked rattlesnake from their freezer, but they didn't tell their guest about the snake. She didn't like snakes. The meal went fine and the lady said she liked American food. Perhaps an hour later the manager thought it was safe to spring the news about the rattlesnake. When the lady heard that she'd eaten rattlesnake as part of her meal, she grabbed her throat, ran to the bathroom and started puking.

On the day-use side of Eastman Lake is a small hunting zone adjacent to the lake. During hunting season, certain animals and birds can be hunted there with a shotgun or bow. I was on the day-use side of the lake one day and a young man found me. He said he had fired his shotgun in the hunting area and his little dog got scared and ran away. He looked all around but couldn't find it. He asked me to keep an eye out and contact him if our staff located the dog. He gave me his name and phone number.

In the days ahead I talked to one of our volunteers about the lost dog; he lived in a trailer on that side of the lake. He said he'd seen the dog several times on a trail and at the dock but the dog was skittish. Days later I was with a contractor in the day-use area and a family drove by and stopped. They were looking for their little lost dog; they wanted to do a search. I showed them the trail where the dog had been seen and wished them luck. About thirty minutes later they drove back and showed me their little Chihuahua. He was shaking and frail after a week in the bush without food, but he was alive. They had walked the trail calling his name and he recognized their voices.

One Spring, a female deer showed up along the day-use side of Eastman Lake with three small fawns. She began a routine of bedding down at night not far from where our volunteer lived in a trailer. During the day she and the little ones would graze in that area and sometimes graze around the restrooms. This continued through the Spring and summer months until the fawns were full grown. What this mother knew was that coyotes don't like people. So she kept her family close to people to avoid the many coyotes in the outlying areas around the lake. All three of her fawns survived and grew up because she was a smart mother.

A Boy Scout leader that I knew told me a scary story. He had taken up archery and became a good shot with a bow and arrow. He and a friend took a hunting trip to a state or federal park. They weren't hunting for bears, but a large rogue bear spotted them from a distance and charged.

The friend saw the bear coming and skinnied up a nearby tree, but the Scout leader took a risk and stood his ground. When the bear got within range, he aimed his bow and let the arrow fly when the bear's front paws hit the ground. The arrow arrived when the bear's chest was exposed and the pain from the arrow stopped the charging bear. One swat from the bear's paw broke off the arrow shaft, then the bear turned and ran back the way it had come.

Both hunters cautiously followed the bear's trail and found it hiding with its back exposed. They put several more arrows into the bear's back to make sure it was dead. The scout leader cut off one of the front paws for a trophy and then the two men went to park headquarters. They informed the ranger staff of what had happened and where to find the dead bear.

Here's a story for dog owners. If you have a dog that barks, or know of someone with a barking dog, there is an easy way to teach that dog not to bark. Go to a dollar store and purchase several plastic spray bottles. Take them home, fill the bottles half full of water, and place them at different locations in the house. When the dog barks, pick up the nearest spray bottle and spray the dog with water. Within a couple of days, the dog will figure out that barking is not good. It works.

Ashes to Ashes

I met fisherman John on the shores of Eastman Lake. He liked to walk the shoreline and fish. I would see John a couple of times a week walking along different parts of the lakeshore, sometimes with other fishermen. He tried to catch anything that would bite. He enjoyed fishing.

One day in the winter it was cold and rainy and John was out there fishing. I stopped and talked to him and another fellow. I asked why they were fishing in bad weather and they said they were catching quite a few panfish. They didn't want to leave because the fish were biting. A couple of hours later I drove past that area and the two men were still out there fishing in the cold.

Weeks later I saw a fisherman who knew John and I asked him why I hadn't seen John for a while. He said that John came down with pneumonia on that cold, rainy day when I last saw him. He was in the hospital. Months later I learned that John was still in the hospital and had gotten worse. Not long after that he passed away.

I was in the office one afternoon and received a phone call from John's wife. She told me who she was and how John hadn't recovered from his bout with pneumonia. She had cremated John's body and wanted to know if it was okay to spread his ashes around the Eastman shoreline. She told me John loved to fish there and it would be a fitting end for him. I told her that the federal government probably has regulations against such, but if she didn't advertise it, who would know? So that's what she did. She visited Eastman Lake and spread John's ashes around the lakeshore, and only she and I and John knew about it.

Refuel

I was patrolling Eastman Lake when a motorized ultralight aircraft flew down from the sky and landed on the park spillway. I drove to where the small craft had set down. The pilot was busy adding fuel to his gas tank. He told me he was low on fuel and needed to fill his gas tank before heading on to his destination. A student park ranger drove up. When the pilot finished fueling, he set himself back in his ultralight and throttled up the engine. The plane started rolling, the wheels lifted off, and up he went.

The next day at work the park manager called me into his office and quizzed me about the airplane. Did I write the guy a citation? The student ranger reported to the manager that I should have cited the pilot for landing an aircraft on federal property. I told the manager it was a no-brainer. The pilot made an emergency landing to refuel his plane; it wasn't a prank. No, I didn't write the guy a ticket for that infraction.

Another aircraft landing involved an Eastman volunteer. He was driving to town and halfway there he saw a low-flying private airplane making passes over the highway. Then the plane set down on the highway a half mile in front of his truck. A lady pilot climbed out of the cockpit and waved her arms at him. He drove to where the plane was parked and she told him she needed his help. Could he flag traffic for her while she added fuel to her gas tank?

The volunteer parked his truck and guided vehicle traffic around the airplane while the lady poured some reserve fuel into her gas tank. She said she was headed north and not certain if she had enough gas in her tank to get to her destination. She was flying into a headwind. When she finished refueling, she buttoned everything down and climbed back in the cockpit. With a clear highway in front of her, she pushed the throttle forward and waved goodbye. Off she went, headed north toward Sacramento.

Desperate People

Behind the dam at Lake Kaweah in California is a free camping area. It has portable restrooms but nothing else, no running water. Some people camp overnight there and I got to know the regulars.

One married couple about forty years old began living there and the story was that he'd lost his job. Their families evidently wouldn't help them so they were on their own, living in a car behind the Kaweah dam. As the days and weeks passed, their situation didn't improve and when I patrolled that area, I sometimes saw her sitting in the car crying.

After a weekend off, I went back to work and talked to the Kaweah campground hosts. They had seen a purple car in the campground parked next to a campsite. When they realized that two people were trying to steal a tent from that campsite, they ran out to confront the thieves. A man and woman got into the purple car and drove away. The camp host got a partial license plate number from the car and gave it to the local sheriff deputy.

After hearing that story, I suspected who the two thieves were but didn't say anything. I checked the license numbers from the primitive camping area which confirmed my suspicion. The homeless couple living behind the dam were gone. Everyone has heard the phrase "Desperate people do desperate things." That's the situation this married couple was in. They were good folks in a very difficult predicament, just trying to survive.

Several weeks later, guess who showed up in the Kaweah primitive camping area again? When I saw their car, I went and talked to the husband. I told him I knew about him trying to steal a tent from the campground and they were no longer welcome in the primitive camping area. He told me they didn't do it and I told him the camp hosts had gotten their license number and passed it on to the local sheriff deputy. Then I told him not to tell me where he was going. The husband realized I knew what had happened but hadn't told anyone. He thanked me for the information and told his wife they had to leave.

I learned from others later that the desperate couple had moved their vehicle location to an orchard some miles away, and the wife still spent time sitting in the car crying.

Topless

It was springtime at Lake Kaweah and the weather was warm. The lake level was up and I was patrolling the recreation areas on a busy weekend. I heard a couple of young men talking about topless female sunbathers so I asked where that was happening. They told me so I aimed my ranger truck in that direction.

From the highway I turned onto a side road where the lake water had risen. There were some vehicles parked and a dozen people around the shoreline. Next to the roadway were five or six ladies sitting on towels, about 25-35 years old. They had on bathing suits but no tops. They were all nice looking, one was a beauty, and none were flat-chested. They were a sight.

They saw my ranger truck go past. I parked and began walking in their direction. People in the area were turning their heads, smiling and watching with interest. The beauty put on a shirt but the other ladies just sat there sunbathing. When I stopped in front of them, the beauty pulled off her shirt, not wanting to be different from the others. None of the ladies were the least bit concerned about being seen topless.

The conversation went something like this: they said they weren't bothering anybody, just taking in the sunrays. I explained that the Corps of Engineers has regulations about nudity on federal property. I didn't make any threats or demands, just asked for their cooperation. Eventually they relented, but it took five minutes of conversation before they put their tops back on.

People in the area were having fun watching and listening to this scene play out. When I walked away, they were chuckling about the park ranger meeting up with the topless sunbathers.

Jet Ski

A contract policeman was on duty at Eastman Lake with me one afternoon. We were both at the day-use dock, looking at a jet ski near the boat ramp. The jet ski was pulled up on shore and had damage to one side. There didn't appear to be an owner around.

Then a vehicle pulled up at the dock, a fisherman I knew. He said there was an abandoned jet-ski trailer along the roadway coming into the park. I drove there and found the trailer, hooked it to my ranger pickup, and drove back to the day-use dock. The policeman and I could see that paint stains on the trailer matched the jet ski. So what happened here? A damaged jet ski is abandoned at the boat dock, and a matching trailer is abandoned several miles down the road.

I checked my warning citations for that afternoon and saw that I had the license number of the vehicle that pulled the jet ski to the lake. The person driving that vehicle didn't pay a day-use fee. I gave that warning citation to the patrolman and we hooked the jet ski and trailer to his police car. The case was now his to solve.

A week later I was notified at Eastman Lake to appear at the Fresno County Courthouse on a certain day and time. I showed up and took a seat outside the courtroom. Other people were there, including a defense attorney. A prosecuting attorney appeared and talked to the defense attorney. The defense attorney told the prosecutor that his client would plead guilty to a misdemeanor but not to a felony charge. When it came time to enter the courtroom, the owner of the jet ski wasn't there. So the prosecuting attorney offered the defense attorney a plea deal: the charge would be reduced from a felony to a misdemeanor. The defense lawyer agreed and the case was settled. We all went home.

I learned later that the owner of the jet ski lived outside of town, and his jet ski was stored in a barn. One of his employees, a teenager, decided to use the jet ski without permission. He took a friend with him to Eastman Lake and they damaged the jet ski.

Afraid to take the damaged jet ski back to the barn, the boys abandoned both the jet ski and trailer.

Both boys were questioned by the police. Only the boy who borrowed the jet ski was charged with a crime. The owner of the jet ski made an insurance claim on the jet ski and trailer, which was paid, so he didn't care about a court trial. The teen who took the jet ski pled guilty to a misdemeanor crime.

Pipe Bomb

I drove into the Eastman campground and a volunteer met me on the roadway. She was living in the campground and pointed to a vehicle that she thought was suspicious. She had the license number written down and when I looked at the pickup truck and license number, there was a problem. I told her to keep an eye on the truck because the guy was a thief. He might be scoping out the campground fee box.

I drove my ranger truck to where the pickup was parked in a campsite. The fellow was changing a tire and with him was a young woman with a small child. When I walked up to him and called his name, he looked up and smiled like we were friends. Then I told him I knew who he was and that he had tried to steal a fee box at the Eastman Lake entrance weeks earlier. The female was holding her young child, and when I began telling her about this guy attempting burglaries at Eastman Lake and nearby Hensley Lake, she broke into tears. I told her the police had confiscated his burglary tools at Hensley Lake and our ranger staff knew all about who he was and what he was. He was furious and denied everything. I wanted him to know that if he had any more burglary plans for Eastman Lake, he would be a prime suspect. When I left, the female was still crying.

The next afternoon I went to work and there were several police vehicles at the office. I was told that a family swimming near the campground dock that morning had found a pipe bomb in the water. They passed it on to a park ranger who called the police. A bomb squad came to Eastman Lake and detonated the bomb in a safe location using a robot.

I had informed the manager and ranger staff the previous day of seeing the burglar in the campground and confronting him. We all knew who likely brought that pipe bomb to Eastman Lake. My guess was that after my chat with his female companion, the guy went home in a rage and made the bomb in his workshop. After dark he traveled back to Eastman with the intent of blowing something up, maybe the campground boat dock. At the dock, he changed his mind and threw the pipe bomb in the water.

When the police detonated the pipe bomb, it had wet gunpowder but it was a live bomb. Wet gunpowder becomes unstable after it dries. This bomb was a serious threat to public safety, but the police made no attempt to investigate who may have made it.

I never saw that burglar at Eastman Lake again, and none of the Eastman staff ever mentioned seeing him again. He took his burglary somewhere else.

Counterfeit Money

A shady character turned up in the Eastman campground with his girlfriend. They camped for two weeks in a trailer. He was a friendly, talkative fellow and said he had a job that allowed him to work his own hours. He never said what his job was, but he left some drug waste products in the bathroom trash one day. At the end of his two-week camping limit, he paid the campground host with cash and left. One of his hundred-dollar bills was counterfeit which was recognized at a bank. The bank notified the police, the police investigated, and a wanted poster was circulated showing the guy's name and face. Eastman Lake and other surrounding lakes and parks in central California were given the wanted poster.

A month later I was patrolling at Eastman and received a radio call from the campground host. I was to come there right away. I drove to the campground and the host told me the poster guy was back. She told me which campsite he and his girlfriend were in. I called the police and told them the story, send cops to Eastman Lake. Thirty minutes later, no cops. Fifty minutes later, two police cars finally arrived at the Eastman campground. I was still there and asked why it took so long. They went to the wrong lake. The camp host and I gave the two officers the wanted poster and informed them that the counterfeiter had just driven out of the campground two minutes earlier. They passed him on the road. Into their cars they jumped and off they went.

I drove to the boat dock and then headed back to the park office, passing the two police cars on the way. The guy's pickup truck was parked in the roadway between the two police cars, and he was lying face down on the road with his hands cuffed behind his back.

The camp host filled me in on details later. The cops searched his truck and then went to the campground to search his trailer. They apparently found drugs somewhere. The man was taken to jail and his truck went with the cops. The girlfriend was not arrested. She spent the night in the campground.

The next day the police called the Eastman office and wanted a home address for the girlfriend. When I went to the campground, she was in tears at the campground office, telling the camp host about her plight. I told her the police wanted a home address for her and the boyfriend, so she gave me an address. I passed that on to the police. She called relatives for help and they came and pulled her trailer out of the campground. We didn't see either of them again.

Prison Crews

When I first took a park ranger job in California, I'd never seen a prison work gang except on TV. I was a rookie ranger at Lake Kaweah when a group of men showed up wearing orange coveralls. Nobody said anything about a prison work crew. They got busy doing trail work, and supervising them were a couple of lawmen carrying guns. This was my first clue. They spent a couple of days improving a trail and I was close enough on one occasion to hear one worker tell another worker not to talk to the "man (guard)".

I spent twenty years working at two federal lakes in California so I saw numerous prison work crews. One lake wasn't far from a women's prison, so Eastman Lake sometimes had women prisoners doing work details.

I gradually developed an opinion about prison work crews, and I first heard this opinion from a manager at Lake Kaweah. He didn't want prison crews anywhere near the office compound or the campground where money was being collected. His view was that inmates will steal tools for weapons whenever possible, and also scope out opportunities for future burglaries. I came to agree with his opinion.

I witnessed instances where other Corps managers allowed prison crews to clean around office and maintenance buildings. No surprise that knives, screwdrivers, and other sharps disappeared. In one case a prison crew spent two days cleaning around a Corps office and maintenance shop. A couple of days later we heard that the prison went on lockdown because of weapons being found. I knew where the weapons came from.

Telescopes

It was an evening work shift for me at Eastman Lake in CA. I did a patrol of the campground dock and found a stargazer there with a telescope. I stopped and chatted with him and looked through his telescope. Then I posed a question to him: what about letting Eastman campers look through his telescope? I could advertise in the campground, and campers could come to the dock and view the planets and stars. The fellow said he could do that and he could also bring a friend with another telescope. So we set it up for a coming weekend. He and a friend brought telescopes to the dock. I notified the people camping and some went to the dock to view the planets and constellations.

The campers enjoyed it and so did the astronomers so we scheduled another session. This time the fellow invited his astronomy club. They all brought telescopes to Eastman Lake on a given weekend evening and I advertised the show in the campground. Lots of people walked or drove to the dock to view the planets and stars. The astronomers trained their lenses on the planets, Saturn, Jupiter, Mars, and the moon, plus some familiar star constellations. Viewers got to see the planets up close.

I kept in touch with the astronomy club after that and scheduled them for more shows at Eastman Lake. It was something different for the campers to see and do, and the astronomers enjoyed interacting with the public. There were lots of questions which made the astronomers feel like experts.

Colored Dreams and Meditation – Story 1

I was about twelve years old when my nighttime dreams changed. They turned active and full of color which was a little scary at first. I didn't like it. Why was this happening; was there something wrong inside my brain? But as months passed and the colored dreams continued, I gradually grew accustomed to them. I was the same person with a different dream pattern; no big deal. Colored action dreams became a regular nighttime feature for me which ceased to be scary.

When I began traveling in a motorhome in the 1970s, computers hadn't yet taken over the world. People were still reading books. I sometimes stopped at book stores and bought cheap books to read. I began reading self-help books like positive thinking. I read a book about meditation that perked my curiosity. The book described an unusual way of meditating to reduce inner stress and tension. I tried it.

The meditative procedure was to sit with eyes closed and mentally lift one hand upward to touch the forehead. It sounded odd but I managed to do it. It took about fifteen minutes, using only my mind and not my arm muscles, to slowly lift my hand and touch it to my forehead. The meditation session ended there. My mind stayed blank and didn't fill with random thoughts or pictures because mentally I was focused on the lifting.

For about a year I meditated like this once each day and it did seem to have a calming effect on me. It wasn't difficult to do so I kept at it. Then I learned about the phenomenon of out-of-body travel. When I started experimenting with trying to project out of my physical body, my interest in meditation faded.

<u>*Write a Book – Story 2*</u>

I was working on a riverboat when a co-worker handed me a book to read. The topic of the book was out-of-body travel. The author, Paul Twitchell, claimed that he could project out of body and other people could, too. The prospect of projecting out of body sounded amazing, but was it really possible? Could I do it?

For the next two weeks I tried concentrating at bedtime in different ways, with no luck. Still on a riverboat, my work shift ended and I laid down in my top bunk bed. I started concentrating on being somewhere outside my physical body. My brain began to tire and then I realized that my physical body had fallen asleep, but mentally I was still awake. So I began imagining myself above my physical body. A roaring noise developed in my right ear and suddenly I was above my body in a world of blackness. I couldn't see my physical form beneath me but I knew where it was.

I wasn't afraid in this situation, but I was confused because I now had no body form at all. My thinking capacity was tremendous, but I had no shape. I was just a thought entity. And I had a pressing problem. I somehow knew that my physical body beneath me had rolled toward the open edge of the bunk bed when I left it. My body was now perched on the edge of the bunk bed, five feet above the floor. That problem needed attention, so I imagined myself back inside my physical form. Instantly I was there. After moving my physical body to a safe position in bed, I tried concentrating again but couldn't project out a second time. The whole experience lasted maybe fifteen seconds, and afterward I was left wondering what happened?

Five weeks later came my second out-of-body experience, and this one I could understand. I was visiting a brother, and at bedtime I began concentrating on being out of body. Growing tired, I slipped into sleep but my brain stayed awake. Here again was the sleep/awake state. Remaining motionless and unsure of what to do next, I thought to myself "I want to leave my physical body", hoping that maybe something or someone could hear me and help me. Suddenly I began lifting upward out of my physical body. A force from below began pushing me up, and I could feel my new energized body separate from my physical form. I could see the ceiling as I rose slowly toward it. When I reached the ceiling, lo and behold, the force continued pushing me upward into and through the ceiling. I could see and feel this happen.

In the weeks and months ahead, I continued my concentration efforts at bedtime, trying to project out of body. My successes were slow in coming. I kept a diary of the occasional out-of-body experiences I did manage to achieve. What I gradually learned was that the best time for contemplation was the middle of the night. If I woke by alarm clock in the middle of the night, got out of bed and went to the bathroom, then went back to sleep contemplating, my chances for out-of-body success were the best. All I needed to do to shift into the inner worlds with some degree of consciousness was to go back to sleep with my eyeballs rotated upward. It might take thirty minutes or ninety minutes for me to drift into sleep doing this, but at the moment of slipping into sleep, something could happen. Chances were good that I would become conscious of being in a solid body in some inner world somewhere. My conscious awareness could be mediocre or very good. Using this contemplative technique, I didn't have to think about or try to leave my physical body; it just happened automatically.

About a year after my first OBE, I decided to write a book. I was keeping a journal of all my soul-travel adventures. My book would follow my path of learning about concentration and contemplation, and also experiencing inner nonphysical worlds. My diary of OBEs was gradually gaining in numbers.

The book took me several years to write. Upon completion, I realized that it wasn't a written masterpiece; it needed serious editing. I put a title to the book, used a pen name, Terrill Willson, and contacted a primary publisher that I was familiar with. In a letter I let the publisher know that the book needed editing and I would accept a standard contract. The publisher agreed to edit and publish the book and sent me a standard contract. Several months later the editing was finished, the book title was changed, and the book went to print. The publisher advertised the book to a wide audience that reached beyond the United States and it sold well. The book is still in print today.

Inner Worlds – Story 3

I first imagined soul travel as projecting out of the physical body into this Earth environment. What I gradually learned was that soul travel encompasses more than just the physical world. OBEs can end up in nonphysical inner planes as well.

When I'm out of body in the inner worlds, I usually have a solid body that feels energized and looks like my physical form. I sometimes project into a world of blackness, but most of my OBEs end up in solid inner worlds that may or may not resemble Earth. My conscious awareness can range from poor to very good. There can be people in the inner worlds that I visit, or strange non-Earthlike beings, creatures, or sights. In short, the inner planes have fascinating things to see.

I'm going to describe here several unusual out-of-body adventures of mine to show how bizarre the inner worlds can be. Keep in mind that these experiences were not scary for me. Few of my OBEs are scary.

I fell asleep one night contemplating and became partially conscious of wanting to leave my physical body. Sleepily I tried lifting my soul body arms; then I felt two giant hands gently clasp my soul body arms together and pull me upward out of my physical form. The hands were huge, each maybe six feet in length, and they pulled me a short distance through darkness to a lighted area. I had vision so I could see the hands; silhouetted against a dark background, they were transparent and without color.

The hands pulled me in front of a white wooden cross which was about five feet tall. Attached to the cross was a golden statue of a man with his arms outstretched. My mental sleepiness was gone by now and my conscious awareness was good, so my excitement about what was happening began to escalate. This caused my mental control to waver and I felt myself begin to slide backwards into darkness. Then came the giant hands again, pulling me back to a kneeling position in front of the white cross. Why this was happening and what it meant I didn't know, but it was exciting. On my knees, looking at the cross and statue, I spoke these words out loud "I respect your religion and your teacher." This statement was meant for whoever was making this happen. Then my overexcitement brought it all to an end. My soul body was drawn backwards into darkness and I ended up back inside my physical form.

The next morning I could still remember what had happened and it was still a puzzle to me. Recently I'd been reading about Padre Pio, the Italian monk whose hands oozed blood for much of his life. I wondered if Padre Pio had somehow been involved.

Here's another strange adventure from the inner planes. After contemplating in the middle of the night and drifting into sleep, I suddenly became conscious of flying in an inner world. My arms were outstretched like glider wings, my conscious awareness was good, and I was about fifty feet above a landscape similar to Earth. While flying along, I could feel a light pressure on the bottoms of my feet which drew my curiosity. What was causing it? Turning my head, I could hardly believe my eyes. Flying behind me, hands holding my heels, was a man I'd never seen before. He looked about thirty years old, dressed in modern clothes, his face and eyes scanning the ground below. And here's the next shocker; he was transparent! I could see through him! I shuffled my feet in his hands to get his attention which made him look up. He saw me waving at him and let go of my feet. Smiling at me, he pointed toward the ground in front of me which I didn't understand. Nodding my head, I flew to where he was pointing. On the ground there, some people were milling about. I asked several of them questions but didn't learn anything.

What I began to realize after this OBE was that people are often with me as helpers when I'm in the inner worlds. If I'm flying, helpers can be flying behind me. If I'm walking, helpers can be walking beside me or behind me. This became a pattern for my soul-travel adventures to come.

My next OBE happened within days and was equally bizarre. After contemplating and drifting into sleep, I became conscious of moving through a darkened sky. It felt like I was being pushed so I turned my head to look. Behind me, glowing faintly against a dark sky, was a yellowish transparent outline of a person's body. I could

162

see the shape of this person who was about twice my size. Reaching back, I tried touching the transparent person but my hands passed through the arms and wrists which felt energized. Then I reached down to my feet where two solid hands were holding my heels. I moved myself to a sitting position on top of the two solid hands, then reached down and squeezed the hands several times. The hands squeezed back. Obviously, this person flying behind me was friendly and providing me assistance. Shortly after this I lost mental control and returned to my physical body so I didn't learn anything more about the fly-behinder.

Several years later came this amazing OBE which happened in the Earth environment. It may sound scary but it was fun.

I was in bed contemplating in the early morning hours and slipped into a sleep/awake state. Realizing what had happened, I mentally spoke these words in my mind "I want to leave my physical body." Waiting motionless to see if anything would happen, an energy force began surrounding my head. Then the energy force began moving down my backside and gradually wrapped around the underside of my entire body.

As the energy gained strength, it pushed me upward out of my physical form. Lying horizontal in my soul body, I was fully conscious and had vision. There was light so I could see the interior of my motorhome. The energy force lifted me to a vertical standing position and turned me around. I could see the front of my RV as the energy pushed me forward about ten feet. Then the energy stopped moving and rotated me again, pushing me back to my bed. There I was lowered backward to a horizontal position and pushed down inside my physical self. Lying motionless in bed, I was wide awake and could remember everything that had happened. The strong energy surrounding my head and body gradually dissipated.

Other odd experiences that I've witnessed over the years include being touched while I'm sleeping. More than once after contemplating or returning from an OBE, I've become aware of a person holding or rubbing my hands or arms while I lay in bed. On one occasion I returned from an OBE and could feel someone massaging my feet and ankles. This touching phenomenon is another reminder that there are parallel worlds to this Earth world that exist on higher energy levels.

Publish a Book – Story 4

It was several years after my soul-travel book was published; I received an envelope in the mail from a friend who had read my book. He sent me a newspaper clipping about a man who had experienced out-of-body travel. The news article described how the man was able to project out of his physical body, and it sounded like the contemplation technique from my book.

After reading that news article, I knew I could write another soul-travel book. I began formatting a sequence of chapters for a second out-of-body book. I was still keeping a diary of all my OBEs which now numbered in the hundreds. I'd learned some new things about soul travel and the inner planes, but more importantly, I'd refined my contemplation technique. Projecting out of body was a little easier and less time-consuming for me now.

The most important part of my new book was how to contemplate and leave my physical body. I'd made some changes. After waking by alarm clock in the middle of the night, I would get out of bed and go to the bathroom. Then I would go back to sleep doing one thing. I would mentally create a feeling of tightness about an inch and a half behind the top center of my head, downward an inch or two inside my head. This isn't hard to do. If I rotate my eyeballs upward, I will feel this tightness inside my head. All I have to do is mentally pull downward on that spot behind the top center of my head, then let my eyeballs relax downward. I want to keep a slight tightness in that area inside the top of my skull until I drift into sleep.

Falling asleep doing this can take me thirty minutes or sixty minutes or maybe more, and whenever my brain loses or forgets that feeling of tightness, I just bring it back. If I can fall asleep feeling this slight tightness inside my head, chances are good that I will become conscious of already being out of body in some inner world somewhere.

Finishing this second soul-travel book took me several years. Included in it were interesting things that I'd learned and seen in the inner planes. After the book was typed, I gave it a title and used my same pen name, Terrill Willson. I sent the book to the same primary publisher that I'd dealt with previously. That publisher returned the book with a rejection letter. So I contacted a secondary book publisher in the Midwest that could do print-on-demand. Print-on-demand was a new book-publishing technology in the 1990s which is less expensive for authors. Print-on-demand enables a publisher to print and sell books one at a time. I paid the publisher several hundred dollars to print my book. The publisher designed a book cover, copied my book into the company printing system, and sent me a batch of books. Then the publisher listed my book for sale on multiple internet book websites. Books purchased were/are printed singly by the publisher and mailed.

Secondary book publishers don't advertise books to the public. They only list books for sale on the internet, then print and mail books that are purchased. So my second book hasn't sold many copies. Few people know about it; it hasn't been advertised. I've purchased copies of the book for giveaway, but sales for the book will be limited. I'm still glad that I wrote the book, however. It was a worthwhile project for me, and the book has useful information for readers interested in out-of-body travel.

Seeing Without Eyes

I watched a television documentary a couple of years ago about gifted children. This group of kids, maybe 8-15 years of age, could see with their eyes closed. To demonstrate this, they all went to the backyard of a house and were blindfolded. All of them could run around the backyard and zigzag between plastic cones. Some of them could read aloud from pages in a book while blindfolded. So how is this possible? How can people read books with their eyes blindfolded? I have no doubt that this documentary was for real, that those youths could indeed see things with their eyes closed.

Back in the 1970s, Stanford Research Institute in CA began experimenting with remote viewing. It was learned that ordinary people were capable of viewing things from afar. Psychics and sensitive people can see pictures of things from the past, and sometimes things happening in real time. They aren't seeing these pictures through their eyes; the pictures are flashing inside the brain, sometimes like a movie.

There are people who can project out of body and see things from the past or present. These images or scenes are not passing through the physical eyes. I can recall occasions when I returned from an out-of-body experience. While lying motionless in bed with my eyes closed, the ceiling above me appeared visible.

Science doesn't yet have an answer for people being able to read books with their eyes closed. How can an Earth image form inside the brain without using the eyes? Does energy flowing through the universe carry pictures and information that the brain can somehow tap in to?

Grandma

I don't remember my dad's parents, but my mom's parents I knew. I remember Grandpa and Grandma Jensen visiting our family when we lived in our big white house in Marshalltown, Iowa. Grandpa Jensen got sick and passed away, but Grandma lived a long life. She stayed with family relatives in Iowa for many years and visited the Warren Willis family several times each year.

Grandma liked our family and everybody liked her. She was a quiet lady. She played games with us and enjoyed being around her grandkids.

When I started traveling around the U.S. in a motorhome in the mid 1970s, I wrote letters to Grandma now and then. She enjoyed getting my letters because nobody else knew where I was. She felt special knowing where her grandson, Keith, was and what he was doing because she was the only one who knew.

I remember where I was when Grandma died. One day I began thinking about her and my thoughts about her continued throughout the day. I didn't know why. I even sat down and wrote her a letter and mailed it. A week later I called home for some reason and learned that Grandma had passed away. Then it made sense; I realized why my thoughts about Grandma had been so strong. She was reaching out to me with family love, and I could feel it.

I called her relatives where she lived and they gave me the story. Grandma had eaten supper that evening and said she wasn't feeling well. She went to her room, laid down in bed, and had a cardiac arrest. It was a quick and peaceful ending for her. She was in her eighties and had lived a full life; her mind was good to the end. Her family celebrated her life and didn't mourn her death. I still think about her and care for her after all these years. She was my favorite Grandma.

Chest Pain

I was working in California and called my folks back home. Dad and I talked for awhile and he told me he had a doctor appointment the next day. He was feeling some chest pain lately along with tiredness and shortness of breath. Two days later I got a phone call at work and was told that dad had heart problems. One of his heart valves was blocked and he needed surgery.

I remembered dad telling me about his chest pain and shortness of breath, and I should have recognized those signals. My park ranger job included first-aid training, and heart attacks are part of that medical course. A person having a heart attack will likely feel chest pain and shortness of breath which can lead to cardiac arrest. Cardiac arrest is advanced heart trauma and life threatening.

So I missed the fact that dad was having a heart attack while talking to me on the phone. A doctor diagnosed his heart problem the next day and scheduled him for surgery. In the years ahead dad had several more heart-related surgeries and lived to be ninety.

When I worked at Eastman Lake in CA, we had an incident involving a group of senior men. They were a social club who met regularly for exercise walks. They chose different locations for their walks and picked Eastman Lake for a trail hike. At the start of their Eastman hike, one member complained of chest pain but decided to go and tough it out. They all began walking a trail overlooking the lake and after a half mile, the fellow with chest pain collapsed. Some of the seniors stayed with him and some walked back and drove to park headquarters. Eastman rangers responded to the scene to find the man dead. The location was problematic so a ranger patrol boat was launched. The man's body was carried down a slope to the lake and the boat ferried the body to the dock.

Here was a case of a heart attack leading to cardiac arrest. Most people envision a heart-attack victim grabbing their chest and falling to the ground. Not true. A heart attack is a prelude to cardiac arrest. Heart attack brings chest pain and weakness due to poor blood circulation in the heart. Cardiac arrest is the next stage of heart failure and very serious, when a person falls to the ground and needs medical attention immediately to survive.

Little Girl Lost

It was afternoon on a busy weekend at Eastman Lake and I got a radio call. A volunteer on the day-use side of the lake reported a little girl stranded. Her family and friends had played and swam that afternoon at the beach area. They went home in two cars and accidentally left her behind.

I drove to the day-use area and the volunteer introduced me to Miranda. She was about three years old and she could tell us her first name but not her last name. We asked what city she lived in and she wasn't sure about that. I made a radio call to the campground hosts and told them the situation. They called the police and asked for a deputy.

The little girl wasn't at all concerned about being left behind by herself; she was smiling and happy. I told her she could go patrolling around the lake with me in my ranger truck and she liked that idea. We drove around the day-use beach and dock area and then to the hunting zone. From there we drove to the entrance fee station. She was having a big-time riding in the ranger pickup, checking things out. Next we drove to the campground dock and group areas and then to the main campground. I parked in the campground and she and I walked around and talked to the camp hosts and volunteers. Everybody loved her and she was having fun meeting new people.

Then came another radio call from the day-use volunteer. A policeman had arrived. I told him to wait there and I would bring the girl to him. I drove to the day-use parking lot and Miranda got to meet the cop. She liked that. I showed the officer where Miranda's family had parked their car at the beach area. He said he would wait there for the mother to return. I told Miranda goodbye and the cop gave her a teddy bear while they waited.

Miranda's mom drove fifty miles home before she learned that one of her daughters was missing. So she drove back to Eastman by herself and was worried when she pulled up beside the police car. Seeing her daughter safe was a relief.

I saw Miranda and her family several more times that summer. They camped in our campground and swam and played at the beaches.

River Rescue

I was patrolling the upper end of Lake Kaweah where the river flows into the lake. It was springtime, the weather was warm, and the river current was flowing strong from the snow melt. I got out of my ranger truck to do some foot patrol and saw two young girls standing on a large rock in the middle of the river. The current on both sides of the rock was swift.

A lady at the shoreline waved to me. The two girls stranded on the rock were her daughters. I asked what happened; how did they get there? She said the girls had been swinging on a tree limb upstream and the limb broke. The girls fell into the water holding the tree limb and were swept downstream. The limb caught on the big rock and the girls managed to crawl up on the rock to safety. Now they couldn't get ashore because of the strong current.

I yelled to the girls to stay where they were; I would get help. I called the local sheriff deputy at Three Rivers and told him what was happening. He asked how far it was from the shore to the rock and said he would be there shortly. In ten minutes he was there with lifejackets and a rope. He was a big, strong guy and he took charge. He tied the rope to a lifejacket and tossed it to the girls. Distance from the shore to the rock was about ten feet. One girl put on the lifejacket, then tied the rope securely around herself. The deputy stepped back and started pulling. The girl came surfing through the swift current to the shoreline. She was fine. She untied the rope, removed the lifejacket, and thanked the deputy for helping her. He told her she was fortunate; he'd seen numerous drownings in this part of the lake.

The deputy then tied the rope to another lifejacket and tossed it to the second girl on the rock. She put the lifejacket on, tied the rope around herself, and the deputy stepped back again. She came surfing across the current and the mother breathed a big sigh of relief. All three of them thanked the deputy again. It had been a close call. If the girls had not been able to crawl onto that big rock after falling into the water, both of them would likely have drowned.

I wrote up an incident report and the Kaweah park manager breathed a sigh of relief after reading it. He had worked at Lake Kaweah for thirty years and seen too many drownings at Slick Rock.

Vandalism

It was after my evening work shift ended at Eastman Lake; I was still at the office and saw some suspicious activity. I confronted four young men who were about to enter an Eastman maintenance compound. Two of the fellows had keys to the gate lock because they were summer Eastman employees. I took all four men to the office and photocopied their identifications, then sent them away. I called the park manager, and the next morning he and I discussed the matter. The manager talked to the maintenance leaderman and then called the area Corps of Engineers supervisor, and the two summer Eastman employees were terminated.

In the following weeks, there began a rash of vandalism at Eastman Lake. Signs were painted which required fixing and cleaning. Damage was done to the Eastman Lake water system at various locations. A Corps quad runner in a fenced compound was hot-wired and driven around. Vandalism happened to the family car of the Eastman park manager at his home in a neighboring city. A grass fire was started one evening between the campground and the Eastman office which brought all the local firefighters to the lake.

Weeks passed and the vandalism continued, so Eastman rangers were scheduled for late night duty. Finally the vandalism came to an end when police arrested one of the four men whom I'd confronted at the maintenance yard. The young man was charged with a crime committed in a nearby city and sentenced to a lengthy jail term. After that, life at Eastman Lake returned to normal.

Murder Trial

A murder trial took place in northern California in 2004 that drew national attention. Scott Peterson was charged with the murder of his wife, Laci, and their unborn child. Laci went missing in late 2002 and her body was found the next year.

I didn't follow the story closely but I saw news about it. Scott was arrested in 2003 after his wife's body washed up on an ocean beach. Following Scott's arrest, his defense attorney initiated a search for a brown van that had been seen near Peterson's home when Laci disappeared. Police knew the owners of the van and did a check of their phone records. A recent phone call had been made from a city in central California. Police called all the lakes and public parks in that area and Eastman Lake received one of those calls. The Eastman campground hosts reported that there was indeed a brown van in the campground. Cops showed up thirty minutes later and verified that the van at Eastman Lake was the missing van tied to the Scott Peterson murder case. Three people were living in the van; two of them were elderly.

I watched the police load that van onto a flatbed trailer for transport to a crime lab. It turned out that the occupants of the van didn't own the vehicle because they were in arrears on their car payments. So the defense attorney for Scott Peterson purchased the vehicle.

After that van left Eastman Lake, I heard no more news about it. Crime investigators cleared the van and the occupants of any ties to Laci Peterson, and the van story turned into a red-herring distraction for the legal defense team. The trial got underway in the Bay area in mid 2004 and lasted until November. The jury found Scott Peterson guilty of murder.

Snow and Ice

It was late Fall and I was traveling through the northwestern states in my motorhome. The weather was turning cold so it was time to head south. I stopped for the night along a main highway and checked a map before going to bed. I decided to try a shortcut road the next day.

Morning came and a light snow was falling. The ground had an inch of snow and I should have headed south on that main road. But I drove a short ways and turned onto the shortcut road. I didn't realize that the shortcut would soon turn into a gravel road.

With a light snow falling, I didn't drive fast. There were a few cars on the road and the snow was a couple of inches deep. Traction on the roadway was getting worse and I came to an uphill incline. Driving slowly up the hill, my tires began to slip and slide so I stopped. This wasn't good. I put my RV in reverse and decided to back down the hill. Rolling slowly backward, I wanted to keep my motorhome in the center of the road but it began to slide. I stepped on the brakes which made it worse; the slide continued toward the left shoulder. The road shoulder was narrow and the bank was steep. As my RV continued to slide, it looked like I would slide to the shoulder and then roll sideways down a steep slope. All I could do was hang onto the steering wheel.

Then the slide stopped, right at the edge of the road. I sat still for a minute, barely breathing, looking at a steep slope to my left. I shut off the engine, secured the vehicle in park, and carefully stepped outside to survey this near disaster. It was then that I saw I was driving on a gravel road. My lateral slide to the left had been stopped by a patch of gravel.

A car drove by and stopped. The driver had a snow shovel so I cleared a path through the snow behind my tires. I asked the fellow to guide me backward to the center of the road. I started my engine, straightened my wheels, and rolled slowly back. When I reached the center of the road, the emergency was over. Now it was a matter of backing slowly down the hill and getting turned around.

The kindly helper had to leave so I thanked him and purchased his snow shovel. I needed it to get my RV turned around in the snow. The snow was still falling when I drove back to the main highway. Feeling tired and relieved, I cooked a meal and stayed the night there. The next morning, I did some motorhome cleanup and headed south on snowy roads. I was fortunate to still have an operational RV.

History/Geography Book

When I began traveling around the U.S. in a motorhome in the 1970s, I had time on my hands. I didn't have much money, but I did have free time. So I started writing a fun book about the history and geography of some of the scenic states I was seeing. I used a map for geography information and visited libraries and book stores for history info.

Then I got interested in out-of-body travel and decided to write a book about that phenomenon. The history/geography manuscript was set aside. After finishing my out-of-body book, I restarted my history/geography manuscript and expanded it to include all the U.S. states plus major countries around the world. That was a big task. When I decided to write a second out-of-body book, my history/geography manuscript was again set aside. After completing and publishing my second out-of-body book, I went back to my history/geography book.

But studying the history and geography of all the U.S. states plus major global countries was a lot of reading and writing. I gradually began to question who would buy the book? Who would want it? Maybe nobody. So why was I writing it? My interest in the book began to fade and I let the project die.

It was still a learning effort for me, though. When I began working in New Mexico as an interpretive park ranger in the 1980s, I knew the history of the region. I had studied the history and geography of all the southwest states, including the native Indian tribes. I could answer questions. And when I later transferred to a park ranger job in California, it helped to know the history and geography there.

Sudden Impact

I can still see the incident in my mind. I was driving my motorhome on a narrow two-lane highway that had a long gradual curve to the left. There were no cars ahead of me, and a long dump truck appeared on the curve coming toward me. The truck had speed and a full load of rocks in the rear box. I was driving about 50 mph and the truck was doing at least 60 mph. As our vehicles closed, I caught a brief glimpse of a rock bouncing upward out of the truck's rear box. Then my front windshield exploded. The driver of the truck probably heard the big rock hit my windshield as he passed by, but he kept on trucking.

It sounded like a cannon blast. My arms jerked the steering wheel which caused the motorhome to swerve left and right. I came close to hitting the truck and then swerving off the road. It took a couple of seconds for me to get past the shock and get my RV straightened out in my driving lane. I slowed my driving speed, trying to mentally regroup. As soon as I could I pulled off the highway and stopped.

Still shaking, I looked around and saw shards of glass scattered everywhere around me. In my lap was a large rock about the size of a baseball. I wasn't hurt; the safety glass in my front windshield absorbed the energy from the flying rock. The windshield had a large hole surrounded by cracked glass. I had no idea that safety glass was that strong. The big rock had to be traveling 100 mph toward my windshield.

But I wasn't hurt and my motorhome didn't crash so it could have been worse. I cleaned up the glass debris and taped a cardboard patch over the hole in my windshield. There didn't appear to be any other damage to the motorhome. My next stop was a glass repair shop where I called my insurance agent.

Best Friend Joe

Every youngster growing up needs a best friend. Especially during school years, students need the support of at least one good friend. Without a best friend, a youngster feels apart from the crowd.

In elementary and middle schools, I had friends but not a best friend. It was eighth grade when I met Joe. He and I were walking back to school after football practice and he told me he was new in school. His family had just moved to town. We talked and he seemed like an "okay" guy. I liked him so we made plans to get together and do something. When I got home from football practice that day, I told my mom that I'd met a new friend at school.

Joe and I started doing things and going places together. He didn't know the students in school so I introduced him around. People liked him, he was a "cool" guy, so I liked hanging out with Joe. This went on from eighth grade through high school. Joe and I became best friends. We knew the most popular students in school and could mix with them. We also knew the less popular groups of students and mingled with them as well. I got to know Joe's family and visited his home often. He, likewise, spent time at my house. So we were a duo during those high school years.

When college came, Joe went to Lincoln, Nebraska, and lived with relatives there. I did a year of junior college in Marshalltown, Iowa, and then went to Iowa State University in Ames for three years. Joe got a bank job in Lincoln and bought a house in the country. I visited him occasionally and spent one summer with him in Lincoln, but we grew apart during those college years. Then he got married and I only saw him a few times after that. By then I was living and traveling in a motorhome and he was married and had a job.

My memories of hanging out with Joe during high school are still colorful, though. We did a lot of things together. He was an important part of my life back then and a good friendship crutch for me to lean on.

Basketball

I listened to the game on the radio because it was played in Las Vegas. It turned out to be the most amazing, most bizarre basketball game ever played anywhere. It was a game for the ages. Highlights of that game can still be viewed on youtube at: Championship Game Highlights: #1 Fresno State vs. #2 Boise State.

The year was 2020, and it was a championship game for the post-season Mountain West women's basketball tournament. Both teams, Fresno State and Boise State, had good teams and were evenly matched. Winner of the game would get an automatic bid to the NCAA tournament.

The game began with Boise State taking the lead. Boise State carried that lead into the fourth quarter but Fresno State came back from a double-digit deficit and tied the game with three minutes to play. Boise State regained the lead but Fresno State swished a long shot in the final seconds to send the game to overtime.

Boise State took the lead in the five-minute overtime. With only 12 seconds left to play, Boise State held a comfortable 78-73 lead. But Fresno State got a bucket, making the score 78-75, and then got a Boise State foul on an inbounds pass. With 5 seconds left on the clock, a Fresno shooter sank the first of two free throws. Now the score was 78-76 in favor of Boise State. On the second free throw, the Fresno shooter missed on purpose because Fresno State needed two points to tie the score. There was a mad scramble for the rebound and a Fresno player got ahold of the ball and lofted up a Hail-Mary hook shot from twelve feet away. The ball went into the basket and should have tied the score with one second remaining on the clock.

But here's where the game unraveled. Just before the Hail-Mary shot was thrown, a referee blew her whistle. She said she heard someone call for a Fresno State timeout. So the Hail-Mary basket was nullified due to the timeout. Then, because Fresno State had no more timeouts, a technical foul was assessed to the

Fresno State team for the timeout being called. This gave Boise State two technical free throws to shoot plus the ball out of bounds with only two seconds remaining in the game. So Boise State won the game 80-76.

Not until the next day, when I watched the game replay on youtube, did I figure out what really happened at the end of that game. When the Fresno player purposely missed the second free throw and players scrambled for the rebound, two Fresno State players came up with the ball. Someone in the audience then yelled for a timeout and the referee heard it. None of the Fresno players or coaches called for a timeout. The referee mistakenly blew her whistle and stopped play. It was an insane ending to an action-packed game that turned a referee miscue into a Boise State victory with seconds left on the clock.

Boise State got the automatic bid to the NCAA basketball tournament, and Fresno State got a bid to the NIT basketball tournament. Neither of those tournaments were played in 2020 because the covid pandemic cancelled all sports for the remaining year.

Caught Cheating

It was an active weekend at Lake Kaweah in CA. I was driving through the campground, about to leave, when I got a radio call from a maintenance worker. He said there was a disturbance at one of the campsites. I turned my ranger truck around and drove to a campsite where a lady was yelling at a man. Her car was parked alongside a campsite which had two men and two women in it, all in their twenties. Both of the females were looking shapely in their bathing suits, busying about with food and drinks. One of the two guys was sitting in a lawn chair. The woman doing the yelling was standing at the edge of the campsite, about the same age. She was telling the man sitting in the chair that she suspected him of cheating on her and now she had proof. She had caught him with another woman.

I parked my ranger truck beside the campsite to make sure the incident didn't escalate. About this time another car drove up and stopped. A man got out and walked over to my open window and asked a question about camping. Then he looked over at the lady shouting. I pointed in the direction of the campground hosts and he went there with his questions. The lady continued yelling at the guy in the chair for another five minutes. Then she took her car keys and slammed them against the side mirror of the car parked in the campsite, breaking the mirror. She told the fellow that all of his stuff would be sitting on her front porch; pick it up and get it gone. She was done with him. Then she got in her car and left.

The two bathing beauties continued busying around the campsite. I asked the two men if they wanted to press charges for the broken mirror and they said not to bother. It wasn't worth the trouble. So everything in the campsite returned to calm and I drove off. My guess was that the fellow sitting in the chair would drive to his ex-girlfriend's home that afternoon. There he would gather his belongings from her front porch, and then move in with his new girlfriend.

Hold Your Horses

It was the end of my work day at Lake Kaweah when I got a phone call from the campground hosts. They reported a problem with a horse at the Slick Rock recreation area and said they had contacted the Three Rivers sheriff deputy. I drove to Slick Rock where I came upon an amazing sight. On the opposite side of the river, a horse was lying upside down in a rock crevice, feet sticking straight up in the air. The horse was apparently alive but couldn't move.

The rider had mistakenly ridden the horse onto a wide domed rock and the horse slipped and fell. It slid down the side of the rock and ended upside down in a crevice. Onlookers were now gathering on my side of the river, and from what I could see, the horse's chances of survival didn't look good.

Horse trailers began arriving on the other side of the river along with a sheriff deputy. Cowboys got busy putting ropes and a large tarp under the horse to try and slide it up out of the rock crevice. They saddled their horses, wrapped the ropes on saddle horns, and several horses began pulling. The horse in the crevice raised a little and then slipped off the ropes and back into the crevice. It was a grim picture.

But the cowboys went back to work. They realigned the ropes under the horse and put a tarp on one side. Then they mounted their horses and gave another pull. This time the horse came sliding up out of the crevice to flat ground. When the horse reached flat ground, it rolled over and jumped up, prancing around like a racehorse. I could hardly believe my eyes. It was a beautiful animal and didn't show any signs of injury.

I talked to the sheriff deputy later about the rescue. He said the rider of the rescued horse was planning a beer fest for the cowboys.

Houston and Isometrics

Years ago when I was traveling, I was in the Houston area and decided to tour the NASA space center. On the day of my visit, the mission control room was full of people. There was a simulated space mission happening, and our tour group could hear the radio conversations. The first space shuttle mission hadn't yet flown; this was a practice shuttle mission. I remember astronaut John Young calling mission control about a problem. Mission control and John Young discussed the problem as our tour group continued on to another part of the space complex. We were taken to see the space shuttle which was being readied for space travel. Workers there were shaking some wires near the engines, trying to locate a wiring problem.

After the NASA visit, my next stop was the Astrodome. The Houston Astros were playing a home baseball game so I went to see the Astros play the Yankees. I bought a cheap seat and the stands were about 25% full. The stadium was impressive and the fans were rooting for the Astros.

Sitting a couple of seats to my left was a fan by himself so we started talking. He told me he was a fitness trainer. I told him I could use some fitness improvement which prompted him to tell me about isometrics. He described for me several simple isometric exercises to tone and strengthen the arms and stomach muscles. No equipment was needed and the exercises required just a few minutes each day. The trainer said that noticeable results would show up in 3-9 months if the exercises are done daily.

Two exercises can tone and strengthen the arms and shoulders. Clasp both hands together and push hard inward for one minute each day. Then push both hands outward against something solid for one minute each day.

To tone the stomach muscles, do these two exercises. Lie on the back and lift the feet off the floor about 45 degrees. Start with thirty seconds each day and work up to a minute. Then, still lying on the back, fix the feet to something solid on the floor and lift the upper body about 45 degrees off the floor. Start with thirty seconds each day and work up to a minute.

The day after that baseball game, I tried these four isometric exercises and began doing them daily. I could see improvement in my arms and stomach muscles within a few months. Today, as a senior citizen, I'm still doing these exercises each day because they work. I spend about six minutes every day keeping my arms and stomach muscles in shape. I would recommend these exercises for everyone; they aren't difficult to do.

Made in the USA
Middletown, DE
18 October 2022

12974494R00104